LET US RETURN TO GOD

Let us RETURN to God

ASRAT ASFAW DABULA

Published by Asrat Asfaw Dabula using Reach Publishers' services,
P O Box 1384, Wandsbeck, South Africa, 3631

Edited by Hazel Hardie for Reach Publishers
Cover designed by Reach Publishers
Website: www.reachpublishers.org
E-mail: reach@reachpublishers.org

ASRAT ASFAW DABULA

asratad@gmail.com

ACKNOWLEDGEMENTS

The Bible says, "And you, being dead in your sins and the uncircumcised part of your flesh lust, hath he quickened together with him, having forgiven you all trespasses" (Colossians 2:13). So may all the glory be to Lord God for helping me; the book takes this shape in the mighty name of our Lord and Redeemer, Jesus Christ.

To give shape to this book and give it a clear and meaningful understanding, brother Girmachew Habte Belay, publisher of *Target* newspaper, has contributed enormous effort for which he deserves my appreciation. My daughter, Weyneshet Asrat, her husband, Samson Alemu, my son, Tewodros Asrat, Mr. Semu Ketema Tefera, and my colleague, Dr Damis Feyisayo Arubay contributed to the costs for the edition and printing of this book, which otherwise would have been impossible for me to get printed. They deserve great thanks for their contribution and direct assistance. They also assisted me in developing ideas that enabled me to publish this book. They have made a very living donation and contribution indeed, and may God bless them, and they are blessed. Brother Yoseph Girma, brother Wasyhun, and many others helped me to find a printing house and distribute it to people; therefore, they all deserve great appreciation.

I want to thank and give great appreciation to those who assisted me in polishing the content by providing additional points to beef up by correcting issues that needed correction. Otherwise, this book wouldn't have taken this shape without their contribution; thus, they deserve great admiration for their commendable work. Let God bless all of you who were involved one way or the other abundantly from His heavenly place.

TABLE OF CONTENTS

Mr. Asrat Asfaw Dabula is a strong person who has put great effort into his work from the time I came to know him, and thus he has put effort into passing his knowledge and sharing with others what he knows and has a good spirit and is the servant of God.

Therefore, now he produced this book *Let Us Return to God*, and it has become one of his excellent books, which I have read. It discusses the life of Christians where they will renew their vigour. The book examines life in the past and how to move forward with the Lord God, what the servants of God need to take care of in walking in line with Him, and how the servants of God should keep order, carefully notice, and open ways of serving Him.

Abiy Assefa Korsa
Eswatini – Ammanuel Evangelical Church (Member of Elders Committee and servant)

Let Us Return to God explains where we stand currently and advises Christianity principles on how to move. The book addresses different points of our lives, thereby showing the right road in life and thus is precious wealth. In addition, the book leads to answering issues we may face daily and assessing the different Christian lives. I thank him for making this noble contribution.

Professor Solomon Worku Kidane
Eswatini University

Brother Asrat Asfaw came to Eswatini (Swaziland) Evangelical church some 20 years back. We have been serving together. I know brother Asrat is an honest, hard-working, and upright servant of God.

I have read *Let Us return to God,* his excellent book. I believe the book is an aid to churches and for the generation. I thank God for helping him prepare this book. I thank our brother for taking the courage to write this book.

The time we live in this 21st century is rapidly moving like technology, and our Christianity is also moving at the same speed; thus, I am afraid it may not have a break to stop it, and it is time we see it stumble like a brakeless car. Christianity is life but not just a talk. Suppose we keep on moving without checking its foundation strength and inquire that we take care more than ever. Only, in that case, there is peace with returning and resting.

Our brother presented his life experience and biblical explanation, which is helpful for seniors, new converts, and those that may come and will enable us to capture essential ideological points. I believe that this book can bring change in life.

Dr Dejene Gelaye
Chairman of Ammanuel Evangelical church

Let Us Return to God, a book written by brother Asrat is a timely book that indicates we need a change in every direction, saints are in different services, and to every Christian fellow, it holds witness that it has an important message. I recommend that leaders of churches and their followers read it because it can bring the long-awaited general renewal at the individual, community, and even parish level. I want to encourage you to read it.

Prophet Yitagus G/ Hiowt
Bole Emmanuel Church servant

FOREWORD

Although this book's preparation is for gospel-believer Christians, it also contains subjects for a wider audience.

Under the Christian faith, some central teachings differ; however, God calls people one way or the other. Therefore, it could have messages to those who do not have a religion or read spiritual books, and those who have the will to know thus, this will help as an eye-opener to everybody.

The purpose of this book is to show the true path of Christ. To those who follow, like the Apostle Paul who wrote to his spiritual child Timothy said, "And that from a child thou hast known the holy scriptures, which can make thee wise unto salvation through faith which is in Christ Jesus" (2 Timothy 3:15) reminds us he advised him how he should live in the house of the Lord.

The book touches upon witnesses and covers vital points; all are not comprehensive, and we may not think all-inclusive to consider as complete. Moreover, as written, "Man lives not by bread only but by the Word of God as well" (Genesis 8:3) should be given priority. This book will encourage you to read reference books, the gospel, and related teachings.

Finally, all the Bible verses quoted are based on KJV version. Thank you. God bless you!

INTRODUCTION

As the word says in Job, "Is there not an appointed time to man upon earth? Are not his days also like the days of a hireling?" (Job 7:1). The life we live in the flesh on earth is challenging. It has ups and downs. But according to God's Word, we must see how we should live in Christ Jesus. It should be according to the gospel taught by the apostles, as mentioned in their messages. What we read in the Old and New Testament says, "All scripture is given by inspiration of God and is profitable for doctrine, for reproof, for correction, for instruction in righteousness" (2 Timothy 3:16).

However, living as an ordinary person, knowing what we read in the holy books, makes it difficult for most Christians in life to keep to the end; moreover, it becomes full of trouble and impatience in their life journey.

As it is mentioned in Ephesians 3:16-17, coming out of such a struggle and a disappointing situation can only be possible through knowledge of the word of God and when we strengthen the inner body through the Spirit, and when Christ lives in us in faith.

It will be difficult for those who did not read God's Word, and did not understand, and those who don't have mindfulness in their journey.

Not obeying happens because of not knowing the Word. Listening to the Word alone is insufficient. The command requires action. "But be ye doers of the word, and not hearers only, deceiving yourselves. For if any be a hearer of the word and not a doer, he is like unto a man beholding his natural face in a glass. For he beholdeth himself, and goeth his way, and straightaway forgetteth what manner of man he was" (James 1:22-24). Moreover, some teach the Word and yet do not practice it. Knowing but not practicing the Word makes the matter even worse.

In this book, more attention reflects the natural thing of making a genuinely Christian life journey. The Christian life journeys are those we notice openly and those that result in weakness in the spiritual life path.

Follow biblical principles and scan them; walking in it can make us lucky, but it might not damage us. Therefore, readers must consider that they will benefit from reading and using it without losing anything. Since it profits with no loss, why not pay sacrifices to use it as a wise person? A brilliant person gives good advice to his property.

God never lies, is not mocked, and never changes His ideas. Therefore, His speeches will pass, as written in His book (the Holy Bible).

Whatever He speaks using His servants in His words has come to pass in the old and our times and are being fulfilled. Therefore, God never leaves Himself without a witness, and He will continue working on this moral duty even in the future.

If we don't live righteously, then when death suddenly comes, the life we lived is because of His mercy, and if it does not enable us to receive forgiveness from God, it will be useless. As it says in the Word, "Well done, good and faithful servant. I will make thee ruler over many things: enter thou into the joy of thy Lord" (Matthew 25:23). If it doesn't help us to enter the Heavenly Kingdom or God's governance, it is just meaningless; it is like the proverb that says "lived and just died" to make people laugh at us.

Hence this book will help us understand His idea; fulfil His Word; walk in righteousness; continue moving according to God's will; follow things tapped from His words; and notice them as an essential guideline.

"All scripture is given by inspiration of God and is profitable for doctrine, reproof, correction, and instruction in righteousness. That the man of God may be perfect, thoroughly furnished unto all good works." (2 Timothy 3:16-17)

PREFACE

Our world is full of ups and downs and complicated walks of life. However, we Christians in this world need to follow specific guidelines/principles that Jesus Christ gave us for this journey. We need to live by these guidelines provided in the Bible by practicing them and following them correctly. In Christianity, as observed, these could be challenging to practice the correct way in life, and our patience might be challenged. It seems it can even lead to hopelessness. To overcome this difficult situation, one needs to be guided by the knowledge of God's Word and strengthen the Spirit to move ahead. For a person who did not read and understand the term, his journey in a Christian life will be arduous. Knowing the Word alone will not be adequate because some people teach it yet cannot practice it. Thus, it will then be a challenging situation.

This book focuses on those strengths and weaknesses in the Christian life journey. It is to create awareness, correct them according to the Word, assist in the walk through the accurate Christian way, and show direction. The book cannot be taken as a complete panacea but as a leading guide to the solutions. Following this biblical experience, the message will not have any adverse effect except benefit the reader. Therefore, while reading, the reader shall consider that it will help but not harm. Consequently, it is wise to pay any sacrifice, if at all it will have, for the benefit you will gain by reading the whole message and using it in life.

God never lies; He is not mocked and does not change His promises. All that He said is true. Therefore, as expressed here, points written in the Bible's words have come to pass in the past, and until this moment, it will continue to be accurate in the future. Suppose we spoil our time unwisely; probably death comes suddenly, and our life ends without preparing ourselves for the heavenly eternal life to inherit the kingdom of God; then it will be useless. In that case, all our effort on earth will be fruitless. This book will help us to come out of such a situation and guide us to walk on the path of God. Therefore, please be calm, focused, and patient to read this book thoroughly by taking each idea and making a deep understanding while trying to associate it with the situation in your life. Take the valuable lessons you get and make them an asset. If there is any point that at first looks not useful, try to look for ways to make it worthwhile for you.

Chapter 1

1. LET US START BY EXAMINING OUR JOURNEY UP TO NOW

According to The Pew Research Center, 2015, in social research, the report says that Christianity is the world's largest religious class, with Christians accounting for 2.3 billion of the world's 7.3 billion population, one third of the world's people.

The morality of the faith's adherents expresses differently because of the changing teachings of the gospel, which is as important as the growth and expansion of <u>Christianity</u>.

From the beginning of the twentieth century until the advancement of technology, they have spread the gospel worldwide and have significantly advanced. As a result, the spread of the gospel increased; on the contrary, the impact of the workforce decreased, and the growing momentum of the gospel aggravated the gospel's reach. Still, events that challenged the gospel are preached and have continued to be a choice in the community.

The gospel of Christ Jesus, who travels through these turbulent circumstances, and the life experience of those His gospel has saved, are similarly confused, and sometimes mixed up.

The continued effort of everyone is also magnifying the foretold events marking the coming of the Lord. Thus, while the Christian congregation has observed and preserved these fulfilments of prophecy, they become an incentive to continue the gospel.

For the world is coming to the last times soon, the starter and fulfiller of all things, God, is bound to fulfil what He foretold in His Scriptures.

In all of this, the gospel says, "All of us who are disciples of Christ Jesus, behold, I come like a thief, happy is he that keeps on the watch and keeps his outer garments clean, that he may not walk naked and expose his shame" (Revelation 16:15). "Therefore, with minds that are alert and fully sober, set your hope on the grace to be brought to you when Jesus Christ is revealed at his coming" (1 Peter 1:13).

Thus, let us see the following topics for us to continue this discipleship instruction.

2. HOW SHALL WE WALK IN HIS HOUSE?

2.1   What should the current situation be?

Christianity is the life of people with strength and knowledge, like the time of the Old Testament when the people of Israel took the book of law that said do this and don't do that. But then, an order with suffering and hardship;

today, life is not like that. Though the journey is not smooth, it is hard.

To know these needs to learn from the beginning what the calling requires. Lord Jesus said this to His followers, "And he that taketh not his cross, and followeth after me is not worthy of me" (Matthew 10:38). He also said, "And when he called the people unto him with his disciples also, he said unto them, whosoever will come after me, let him deny himself, take up his cross, and follow me" (Mark 8:34). In Luke 13:24 it says, "Strive to enter at the strait gate: for many, I say unto you, will seek to enter in, and shall not be able." However, its invitation has ups and downs in its journey.

The real unadulterated gospel preaches the life of rest in Christianity, but the way in life does not show it is comfortable. Since it is hope, Christianity involves a cross; it has sufferings in its life journey.

As we live in this world, we wait tomorrow with hope; otherwise, we do not know what will happen tomorrow or what we will face; none of us will be sure of it. Why? Is it because the future becomes unknown to us? Among creatures, none of us would tell what happens for sure in the next second, hour, day, week, etc. Meteorology forecasts during news broadcasts saying, 'It might be like this or like that,' but will not tell what would happen because of this. Since the next moment is unpredictable, the Lord has taught us the following:

"Go to now, ye that say, today or tomorrow we will go into such a city, continue there a year, and buy, sell, and gain.

What does the current situation look like? Whereas ye know not what shall be on the morrow. For what is your life? It is even a vapor that appears for a bit of time and then vanishes away. For that ye ought to say, If the Lord will, we shall live, and do this, or that." (James 4:13-15)

Therefore, as we live as carnal in this world, we must live as if we may suddenly die; thus, we should be ready to go to our eternal home.

Like the times of Noah, people were not saying, 'We still have time,' but were not able to think if we slag, we might not be able to get time (even to confess), we might not get a chance. For example, some people die in an accident suddenly. If such people are going to prepare early enough, they would have been lucky; but it would be a significant loss if they were not. If they did not finally qualify for what they want to achieve, then what they have struggled with in their lives would be in vain.

Since our carnal body is weak, we cannot make God happy in our life journey; thus, we must be cautious. Therefore, the people of God need to check and ensure they consistently repent daily.

Respecting God's Word must be day-to-day practice checking oneself as the Apostle said to the people of Corinthians in his message:

"For this cause many are weak and sickly among you, and many sleep. For if we would judge ourselves, we should not be judged. But when we are judged, we are chastened of the Lord, that we should not be condemned with the world." (1 Corinthians 11:30-32)

When the flesh gets defeated with these worldly needs, it will then be without the protection and help of the grace of the Lord. Unless it returns immediately, the person might separate from the Lord. Separation then is a challenging situation, but the Lord said a graceful word giving us hope saying, "Be brave, for I have won the world" as He says in John 16:33: "These things I have spoken unto you, that in me ye might have peace. In the world ye shall have tribulation: but be of good cheer; I have overcome the world."

To overcome the world does not mean doing what you wish, but He told us that if we live according to His commandment, He will support us with His grace.

All Christians need to obey and live according to the Word with the grace the Lord will give us.

As it says in the Word, "For it is God which worketh in you both to will and to do of his good pleasure." (Philippians 2:13)

Grace means the power of God that helps us through divine means to do what we cannot do in the flesh on our own. To get this opportunity, we need to walk before God in righteousness and holiness, but this is possible with what Jesus Christ did, believing in that and living accordingly. Living according to the Word is likely not because of what we do but because of what Christ did on the Cross for us; with the righteousness, we received from Him and Holiness, we can appear before God and walk with it.

For this reason, God will not avail Himself and will not work where there is no righteousness. But unfortunately, His behaviour doesn't allow Him to do it.

God is almighty. There is nothing impossible to Him. However, for example, when people know their sins, confess, and return from their sinful ways, He can't say, "I will not forgive you." It doesn't matter how much man sins, He can't hate the man but only the sin. Therefore, we shall not disappoint God for these beautiful characters He has. But much as He is merciful, He can also be angry, and no one can save anyone from the destruction; His wrath is also devastating.

When King David committed a sin and God gave him the choice of punishment selected through the prophet, David opted to get the opportunity to fall in the hands of God; because he thought God might forgive him. He was then able to save his people from the severe punishment that would come upon him and his people by attack or famine.

"And David said unto God. I am in a great strait: let me fall now into the hand of the Lord; for very great are his mercies: but let me not fall into the hand of man." (1 Chronicles 21:13)

Our Lord defeated the devil on the Cross of Calvary after giving Himself willingly to pay the price for our sins, though He did not commit any sin that will take Him to that level of punishment. Hence, we shall live as free people, set free. Let us look at the following questions to examine our current situation since it will help us check ourselves.

3.   WHAT IS GOING ON IN OUR LIVES TODAY?

Let us check how we live everyday life in our Christian lives. Are we going to live apart, sanctified, in righteousness, or are we going to pretend to be holy and righteous men? We should do the right thing by being honest with ourselves when we answer this question. What does the reproof of the Holy Spirit speak to us? If we don't live up to and respect His Word, the problem or responsibility will not be that of church leaders or someone else's. Salvation is only for oneself, not for a father, mother, relative, or anyone else. Some may think this foolish. Therefore, we need to scour ourselves and correct ourselves for our good.

4.   WHAT DO WE FEEL ABOUT OUR CURRENT LIFE?

What we feel about ourselves and what people talk about and think about us are primarily different. Most of the time, it is the opposite. The truth is in the individual, but only the way people express themselves might seem right by looking at the external condition. The decisive situation is examining those opinions from their perspective and telling us if they are proper or mistaken. Leaders must check their views against God's Word, whatever it is. Therefore, when a Christian wants to investigate their life, the measurement shall be the Word of God. Above all, self-criticism must be practiced and noticed to correct and find guidance to save us from making mistakes. When we hear the Holy Spirit witness to our inside (to our Spirit) to protect us, we shall obey, which is very important.

If we have a comfortable and lavish life in this world, stopping and checking our way is very important. As the Word says, if you feel you are walking correctly, you must ensure that you don't fall necessary. "Wherefore let him that thinketh he standeth take heed lest he falls." (1 Corinthians 10:12)

Especially if we find people who will boldly tell us our mistakes, we should understand these are the real loving people. Father punishes his child for a mistake because he loves the child. He doesn't want his child to be spoiled, for he loves him. We often observe that people hate those who tell them their mistakes, consider them enemies and quarrel with them. Not accepting critics is a great mistake and misunderstanding.

"A scorner loveth not one that reproveth him: neither will he go unto the wise." (Proverbs 15:12)

"He that refuseth instruction despiseth his soul: but he that heareth reproof getteth understanding." (Proverbs 15:32)

5. HOW STRONG IS OUR RELATIONSHIP WITH THE LORD?

Among practical things, we should question our relationship with God through the Lord by asking for help from the Holy Spirit. If we live by walking upon the hopes we received written in the Bible, and if we are walking considering the outstanding debts we have for God, as He has loved us before, our heart should see that Aba Father lifts our joy and love.

To be followers of Christ should be above merely calling His name, but we must reveal ourselves day-by-day practicing His teachings. Therefore, if I am a follower of Jesus Christ, becoming one who does not do those things by doing what He did with faithfulness in following Him would be a mistake.

Some Christians who were in Cretian's claim are followers of Jesus Christ group; they talked as if they knew God and called after Jesus Christ who spoke but did not live the life; Paul reprimanded them strongly and advised Titus not to follow them as written in the Word as follows:

"For there are many unruly and vain talkers and deceivers, especially they of the circumcision: Whose mouths must be stopped, who subvert whole houses, teaching things which they ought not, for filthy lucre's sake. One of themselves, even a prophet of their own, said, The Cretians are always liars, evil beasts, slow bellies. This witness is faithful. Wherefore rebuke them sharply, that they may be sound in the faith; Not giving heed to Jewish fables, and commandments of men, that turn from the truth. Unto the pure all things are pure: but unto them that are defiled and unbelieving is nothing pure, but even their mind and conscience defiled. They profess that they know God, but in works they deny him, being abominable, disobedient, and reprobate unto every good work." (Titus 1:10-16)

As the growth of humans from infanthood is not limited to remaining as it was at birth time and date, spiritual development will not stay at the same level after being born again in our relationship with God. Through the word, prayer, and brethren fellowship, we can grow and continue to grow. We shall not have stunted growth that remains the same level as some children may have fulness of God. No one will stop at a certain level.

"That he would grant you, according to the riches of his glory, to be strengthened with might by his Spirit in the inner man; That Christ may dwell in your hearts by faith; that ye, being rooted and grounded in love, May be able to comprehend with all saints what is the breadth, and length, and depth, and height; And to know the love of Christ, which passeth knowledge, that ye might be filled with all the fulness of God." (Ephesians 3:16-19)

For this to happen, the ministry of fellowship in the church has its role to play, but each believer must be diligent in knowing and practicing the spiritual things that are part of the fellowship in life. It should also be a priority.

When this happens to a fully-fledged believer in his relationship with the Lord, it will be strengthened and remarkable. Time, conditions, incidentals, new events, and life experiences will enable him to have an unchangeable relationship with the Lord.

As a Christian, whatever duty does assign to one in the church, he should accept without making hierarchical ranks (high or low) to the service and participate in any field with love and serve with total willingness. When a Christian is with the Lord and confronted with tasting situations, he must have confidence in the Lord's capability to save him. Therefore, he must stand firm and attach himself to the Lord. Therefore, Lord is the Lord of victory and will give him His grace to withstand the situation.

"There hath no temptation taken you but such as is common to man: but God is faithful, who will not suffer you to be tempted above that ye are able; but will with the temptation also make a way to escape, that ye may be able to bear it." (1 Corinthians 10:13)

"Wherefore seeing we also are compassed about with so great a cloud of witnesses, let us lay aside every weight and the sin which doth so easily beset us, and let us run with patience the race that is set before us, Looking unto Jesus the author and finisher of our faith; who for the joy that was set before him endured the cross, despising the shame, and is set down at the right hand of the throne of God." (Hebrews 12:1-2)

6. DID WE GROW WITH OUR SPIRITUAL LIVES?

In spiritual life, growth, even though it is not visible as physical growth, will be displayed in many ways. Additionally, the individual can feel more when spiritual growth occurs within him instead of outside observers. It becomes visible in life by becoming obedient to the word, actioning, sharing with others, accepting Jesus Christ as his Saviour after he believed, spiritually taking Jesus Christ as head of his life, and revealing these in all aspects of his life.

Holy Spirit can be visible with self-control, love, humility, wisdom, being a model, patience, calmness, obedience, and endows power of characters as a grownup Christian. Therefore, these mentioned conditions will become well expressed in Him.

Let us check how we are living in our day-by-day Christian lives. We shall answer questions later. Try to reply honestly and earnestly without lies because it is for our benefit. How do we respond to the warning of the Holy Spirit that lives in us? Are we living for the sake of God, alienated with holiness and righteousness, or are we trying to satisfy our flesh and do whatever we wish, yet try to look holy and righteous before people? Are we complying according to the Word? If we do not respect His Word and live according to His Word, the problem will be ours, not church leaders, or any other person's. Salvation is for oneself, not your father, mother, relatives, or another person. Some people might think foolishly like this. Therefore, we shall try to check against such and correct them to our advantage.

"Put on, therefore, as the elect of God, holy and beloved, bowels of mercies, kindness, humbleness of mind, meekness, longsuffering." (Colossians 3:12)

A spiritually grown Christian will be refrained from being spontaneous and sensitive. But the one who did not grow spiritually will have a problem with anger, aggressiveness, rushing for action, hatred, gossip, theft, adultery, insult, jealousy, and other flesh weaknesses. How lucky is a person who is free from such? When talking about fleshly sin, the Apostle lists the following:

"Now the works of the flesh are manifest, which are these; Adultery, fornication, uncleanness, lasciviousness,

Idolatry, witchcraft, hatred, variance, emulations, wrath, strife, seditions, heresies, Envying's, murders, drunkenness, revellings, and such like: of the which I tell you before, as I have also told you in time past, that they which do such things shall not inherit the kingdom of God. But the fruit of the Spirit is love, joy, peace, longsuffering, gentleness, goodness, faith." (Galatians 5:19-22)

Therefore, we need to run away from among those listed fleshly weaknesses. As mentioned above, the fruit of the Holy Spirit, thus, must follow up in life, for the above points to reveal in life are essential.

7.   WHAT SIGNS DID WE SEE ABOUT OUR MATURITY?

One of the spiritual maturity signs in life is a developed strong faith, enabling one to perform wonders and miracles by calling the name of Lord Jesus Christ. In addition, the honour and respect a believer gives to Jesus Christ's name with faith will significantly impact the service he provides.

A faithful Christian humbles himself; he is meek and obedient; he doesn't investigate situations and time to serve but does his part any time. When spiritual maturity comes, all anointing grace will be revealed in the believer's life more than ever and operate mightily. The signs the Lord spoke about will follow the individual in his life and service.

"And these signs shall follow them that believe; In my name shall they cast out devils; they shall speak with new tongues." (Mark 16:17)

Living on this earth without shame and criticism could be challenging, but it is possible for those who lean on the Lord. They can live with people; they have a forgiving heart; even if saints are hurt, they still ask for forgiveness from the person who hurt them. Being without blame is a sign that will show one believer has reached spiritual maturity. Stephen is one good example of this in Acts 7:60, "And he kneeled down, and cried with a loud voice, Lord, lay not this sin to their charge. And when he had said this, he fell asleep."

8. DO WE NOTICE THE OBSTACLES WE FACE?

We must examine and search carefully for tribulations and tests in how Christian's travel. We need to know the cause, review the sacrifices required, and see whether we need to retreat or boldly face the best option. God does not test man. As the Word says in James 1:13, "Let no man say when he is tempted, I am tempted of God: for God cannot be tempted with evil, neither tempteth he any man."

The test can happen in two ways; this could be from either flesh or Satan. When one is defeated and moves to satisfy his fleshly needs without examining what he does is not in line with God's words, man will fall into fleshiness. On the other hand, what comes from Satan would be considered when Satan tests knowing the fleshly weaknesses of humans very well, and Satan will facilitate conditions favourable to sin. Any man can fall into the trap easily if he moves without checking. Both are sinning that God will judge; that is, eternal death. Because God said, "The price of sin is death" (Romans 6:23). The solution to this is to run away from sin (refuse).

"For the wages of sin is death; but the gift of God is Eternal life through Jesus Christ our Lord." (Romans 6:23)

"Flee also youthful lusts: but follow righteousness, faith, charity, peace, with them that call on the Lord out of a pure heart." (2 Timothy 2:22)

9.   WHAT COULD BE THE SOURCE OF OUR TEST?

As explained above, the source of sin could be from two directions; those that emanate from one's flesh may not be difficult to differentiate and notice yet we tend to undermine them. Thus, those who continue to live under the will and control of their flesh can be considered worldly people. Romans 8:5 says, "For they that are after the flesh do mind the things of the flesh, but they that are after the Spirit the things of the Spirit."

Always fleshly committed sin will not prove spirituality. A spiritual person must be far from such. During this time, people expose themselves to their internal feelings by wrongly interpreting and understanding the word and eventually end up inviting danger to themselves. Then sin will override and bear eternal death. No 'Christian' who goes this way shall cheat himself to be a Christian. Directly violating, knowing right and wrong from the Bible but not respecting it is sin itself.

"But as he which hath called you is holy, so be ye holy in all manner of conversation; Because it is written, Be ye holy; for I am holy." (1 Peter 1:15-16)

Being scared of the Word cannot be used as an excuse. Being devoted to God coming from the old self of the evil world would be our idea. Similarly, we must reflect that we are dedicated to God if we have to show we agree with His behaviour. The measurement of holiness is not with us; it says in 1 Samuel 2:2, "There is none holy as the Lord: for there is none beside thee: neither is there any rock like our God." Also, Revelation 15:4 says, "For thou art holy."

Concerning us, God said in 1 Peter 1:16, "Because it is written, Be ye holy; for I am holy." We understand that the measurement of Holiness is God himself that man cannot be. We know that the Bible says in 2 Corinthians 10:12, "For we dare not make ourselves of the number or compare ourselves with some that commend themselves: but they are measuring themselves by themselves, and comparing themselves among themselves, are not wise." He is a foolish one who compares himself with himself. To whatever level our holiness becomes high, our righteousness shall be weighed only by God must be clear. As we notice in the prayer, when our Lord prayed, we understand when He said, "Sanctify them through thy truth: thy word is the truth" (John 17:17). The way God revealed Himself and how we shall have a relationship with Him is this way. The way God revealed Himself and how we should associate ourselves with Him is displayed this way. That is why Jesus explained that He is the truth. "Jesus saith unto him, I am the way, the truth, and the life: no man cometh unto the Father, but by me" (John 14:6). It also says in John 1:8, "Nobody was able to see God, but Jesus narrated."

He revealed Himself through the truth of the word. Therefore, showing what he wanted of man and what God said about himself will help us separate from our bondage and enable us to align with God.

Therefore, holiness is not to be separated from God, but it is refraining from sin, without shame or criticism. Of course, anything that happens in human life might not be visible to the human eye, but even if someone secretly does something, he cannot hide from God.

Therefore, our holiness shall not be before man; it is the situation where we keep ourselves away from sin, where there are no people who would ask us why this or that, where there is no man to rebuke us. Therefore, holiness is an issue of the heart. Nobody plays hide and seek, but one should give oneself to God because nothing can hide from God. He knows that because the eyes of God can easily see everywhere, any spot.

"For the eyes of the Lord run to and from throughout the whole earth, to shew himself strong in the behalf of them whose heart is perfect toward him." (2 Chronicles 16:9)

"For God shall bring every work into judgment, with every secret thing, whether it be good, or whether it be evil." (Ecclesiastes 12:14)

"He revealeth the deep and secret things: he knoweth what is in the darkness, and the light dwelleth with him." (Daniel 2:22)

"Fear them not therefore: for there is nothing covered, that shall not be revealed; and hid, that shall not be known." (Matthew 10:26)

Under the sun, whatever happens to us in our lives is clear to our Almighty God. Thus, we must live without shame and criticism, and we must renew our life through confession whenever we find a weakness.

"For the word of God is quick, and powerful, and sharper than any two-edged sword, piercing even to the dividing asunder of soul and Spirit, and of the joints and marrow, and is a discerner of the thoughts and intents of the heart." (Hebrews 4:12)

10. HOW DO WE CONSIDER OUR TESTS?

The level of all tests is not the same or will not be the same if you see the weight, duration, origin, and effect. But it helps us in our effort to investigate the test and the way out.

A proverb says, "Knowing the problem is halfway to solving the problem." Therefore, if we know the source of the problem, then it will not be challenging to find the solution.

As Christians living in this world, it would be a great mistake if one thought they would be outside of being tested.

The devil's task is to stress a Christian's day and night to make them fall into his trap. Then, Satan will try to defeat Christians by preparing tarps on their way.

The other test is what comes to a Christian when he creates a problem and falls into the devil's trap. Take the sin of adultery as an example. Again, by not being exposed to this sin can help avoid any situation facilitating such.

Those unmarried males and females should not stay alone without other friends joining them even if they believe they will not succumb to sinful temptation. It doesn't matter how strong they think they are in faith; after staying long together without being accompanied, being only the two of them alone, they may not resist the sexual feelings that the flesh might develop.

Therefore, they may fall into sin most of the time because of staying together in a closed room, which is conducive to the problem.

If a man and woman are not married when they want to pray together, they must constantly find at least one other person to be the third one to join them. Even if they are fiancés, they should not be left alone in a closed room to pray. It shouldn't be. Before marriage, if they are left alone to pray in a secure room or hidden location, they invite themselves to sin.

Therefore, we need to notice those situations that expose us to temptation. Then, after understanding them, we should try to protect ourselves from falling into sin and regretting it later.

Hiding or concealing sin and not returning through confession will have dangerous consequences. But, on the other hand, acting enough and noticing as early as possible protects us from falling into a sinful situation, thereby avoiding regret or suffering from the consequences that could come later on.

11. WHAT ACTION SHOULD WE TAKE TO COME OUT OF THE TEST?

This worldly test comes with many ups and downs waiting for us. The test can happen in different ways because this test can come from Satan, how we live, from other people, because of some situations, or from the flesh. We can cite some examples. There is no doubt that the enemy's work is behind most tests.

However, the Lord said, as written in the book of John:

John 16:33, "These things I have spoken unto you, that in me ye might have peace. In the world ye shall have tribulation: but be of good cheer; I have overcome the world." Therefore, it doesn't allow us to suffer from a test we can't win.

"There hath no temptation taken you but such as is common to man: but God is faithful, who will not suffer you to be tempted above that ye are able; but will with the temptation also make a way to escape, that ye may be able to bear it." (1 Corinthians 10:13)

You may sometimes feel that a temptation is too over-powering for you to bear, but that's a lie from Satan. God has promised never to allow more on you than you can handle. He will not permit any temptation that you cannot overcome.

A person will feel guilty without anyone accusing him because the Spirit reprimands him with a guilty conscious-ness. Therefore, since the Holy Spirit makes a reprimand to our minds, it comes at any time. Consequently, we shall comply with it.

When we face tests, there is the inside being that would tell us or transfer a message. God created man in His image, especially in a much more attractive manner, with particular attention.

We can resist internal and external problems naturally. For this, when our inner body feels sick, an antibody would fight back unless the problem is above its resist-ing capacity.

When the problem is above our body's tolerance capacity, it will show signs of fever, subtle ache, headache, dysen-tery, and vomiting, and it can begin to show a sign of dis-ease. At this time, we need to get assistance from a medi-cal service. Getting medical assistance does not mean we should not pray and ask the Lord whichever way He wants to address our problem. The healer is the Lord in any case because He also gave the knowledge to doctors.

One of the external relationship problems we may have with another person is when it becomes aggressive, angry, disappointed, and being suppressed forcefully (a fight).

As Christians, when someone challenges us to fight, even if we are strong enough to fight back, that Christian life, the life we have taken in Christianity, does not allow us. Because it says in the Word:

"And if thy right eye offends thee, pluck it out, and cast it from thee: for it is profitable for thee that one of thy eyes should perish, and not that thy whole body should be cast into hell." (Matthew 5:29)

"Not rendering evil for evil, or railing for railing: but contrariwise blessing; knowing that ye are thereunto called, that ye should inherit a blessing." (1 Peter 3:9)

If a person slaps you on your right cheek and then asks the person, "why did you slap me?", your heart is full of anger. If you are angry because of the slap on your cheek, and you ask why the person did this to you, it means that you are one of the people that try to protect their rights on their own. Therefore, the way you reflect and respond will be full of anger. In any case, you asked what happened to you and what will happen to you is not what a Christian should do.

It is better to respect the Word and get hurt than be outside the Lord's commandment; maybe the damage is on the perishable flesh, but it will be valuable and profitable to our home in heaven. Therefore, when we have a problem with our brethren and sisters in the Lord, we should remember (as it says in Matthew 18:15) "Moreover if thy brother shall trespass against thee, go and tell him his fault between thee and him alone: if he shall hear thee, thou hast gained thy brother."

"And if he trespasses against thee seven times in a day, and seven times in a day turn again to thee, saying, I repent; thou shalt forgive him." (Luke 17:4)

If your brother trespasses against you, it is not something new in the world. It is common to trespass against one another. However, it may not happen all the time. It may happen once in a while. The Lord has shown us what we should do in such instances. It says, "criticize him when you are alone" (as we find in Matthew 18:15). If somebody trespasses, you must, first of all, tell them directly. Accordingly, this is the word we need to know. When you and he are alone, show him his mistake.

Suppose your brother trespasses; do not talk of his mistake to other brethren and sisters before telling him to correct it. Do not even go to any responsible Church brethren. Believers need to know him openly if he refuses to accept his mistake. If your brother trespasses, first, what you must do is tell him. If sinners respect the commandments, we shall believe that repentance might solve most or part of the church's problems.

We see today that when one brother trespasses on another, the issue reaches those who are not aware before the individual knows it. Then everyone knows the case. Then we observe the other brother who is hurt spreading the news to everyone he can reach, showing weakness. It is weak that it goes around and spreads such information. He is soft and circulates the notice that someone has hurt him. If someone cannot talk to the person who hurt him, it means that person's conscience is weak and devastated. This type of person can only go around and gossip. He doesn't have the strength to speak face to face at all. So, gossip and hearsay are blowing and spreading an evil, sinful practice. We should be careful of our brothers' and sisters' mistakes and not tell others. The first person to know must be the person who made the blunder. It should not be any other person. Children of God must learn this; the church must come free from such problems.

No reason is enough to run away from asking for forgiveness or forgiving others by justifying their actions or wrongdoings. Reasoning happens literally from not knowing the word or not believing in it. The one who doesn't want to forgive cannot get forgiveness, as the Word says:

"But if ye forgive not men their trespasses, neither will your Father forgive your trespasses." (Matthew 6:15)

"And if he trespasses against thee seven times in a day, and seven times in a day turn again to thee, saying, I repent; thou shalt forgive him." (Luke 17:4)

As mentioned above, no option is available except forgiving; if we can't do this, then it is a matter of not understanding the word. We have only one choice: to forgive those who trespassed against us. If one cannot forgive, one will be ignored by the Lord and <u>must live knowing this</u>. If so, then what advantage does Christianity have for him? Why should he then be called Christian?

Therefore, to come out of this trouble, we need to walk, taking decisive action by giving it into the hands of the Lord, who can dismiss it and help us forgive others. Holding resentment and walking with it doesn't take us anywhere. In Ethiopia the elders say, "Coughing when you are stealing and praying while having resentment will not help."

We understand that the test is inevitable and is a day-to-day event; thus, we value what action we take to avoid it and determine the remedy that makes us successful or fail.

Sometimes, we may consider avoiding the problem by leaving our location and moving to another area. Going places and running away may not be necessary for such situations. Get up and close the TV set. Don't cooperate with people who gossip. If you were watching a movie, then stop it and get out. To be not bitten by bees, get away from bee areas. The best way is to make sure your focus is changed as much as possible.

12. HOW READY ARE WE TO SERVE GOD?

The word 'service' in Greek is *diaconay*. *Diaconay*, however, doesn't have a straightforward meaning. It has many different meanings.

Similarly, in the Old or New Testament, 'service person' has been translated in many ways. Many times, 'service person' means 'being a servant'. In English, 'server' and 'servant' give different meanings based on how they are expressed and may have meaning in expressing the status of people; however, the difference in the meaning in the original language is unclear. Many times, the word can take a different meaning. If there is a difference, it is how we use it. If we see the word 'servant', it is used to look into it from the perspective it may mean what someone is doing. The first meaning is to be obedient to the boss (as we find in Romans 6:16-18; and Ephesians 6:6-7. The last word shows giving service to others as mentioned in Matthew 20:28; Luke 10: 40; and Romans 12:7.

We shall follow how it works in churches in different ways.

Many Christians remain served as their option; thus, they tend only to receive service and do not participate in the church.

Every Christian has a calling when he accepts the Lord. Often, we observe people running away from giving any service to the church, with many different reasons why. On the other hand, some have the anointing and the will, yet church pastors/leaders may not invite them for any service.

Likewise, those assigned to serve may not give the service loyally. In these three scenarios, there is a striking difference and problem. No performers are those who bury their talent, and those that want to serve and yet are not allowed for many reasons may move into disagreement and conflicting situations. In contrast, those who did not respectfully carry on their assigned duties become obstacles to the service of the house of God.

We must give a solution to each without restriction. Is it a better and even excelling choice for those Christians serving God? Is there any reward given to the Lord who gave us His life and enabled us to get eternal life, or is there anything better we can do? Who do we want to serve if we are not serving this God?

Christians of the New Testament are servants of God.

1 Peter 2:9, "But ye are a chosen generation, a royal priesthood, a holy nation, a peculiar people; that ye should shew forth the praises of him who hath called you out of darkness into his marvellous light."

Except for those serving the Lord already, all Christians must serve God one way or the other. Since God has limitless service opportunities, they must think and act to serve God with whatever they can (as we find in Ephesians 6:5-8; Colossians 3:23). This service should not only be in religious services. Jesus counts whatever service you give every day as it is for Him, even if the service-giving people do not realise it (as we find in Matthew 25:35-40).

On the contrary, people can be in services that seem to serve the Lord yet take it as their own. However, the service from these people is for their advantage, seeking personal benefit and not serving the Lord at all "No man can serve two masters: for either he will hate the one, and love the other; or else he will hold to the one, and despise the other. Ye cannot serve God and demon" (as we find in Luke 16:13) "Serving Christ means helping others. Those that serve others have a reward from God". As we find in Matthew 6:24: "But Jesus called them unto him, and said, Ye know that the princes of the Gentiles exercise dominion over them, and they that are great exercise authority upon them. And whosoever will be chief among you, let him be your servant: Even as the Son of man came not to be ministered unto, but to minister, and to give his life a ransom for many." As we find in Matthew 20:25-28 and 23:11-12: "But he that is greatest among you shall be your servant." Of course, this does not mean Christians serve to get compensation from God. On the contrary, they should know they give the service because it is their responsibility. As we find in Luke 17:10: "And they that were sent, returning to the house, found the servant whole that had been sick." However, God has vowed to reward those who serve Him as they help Him understand their responsibility accordingly, which will be to the extent of His kindness and honesty. We see this in Matthew 25:21; Luke 19:17; Hebrews 6:10; and Revelation 2:19, 26.

Church elders should assign church members (from the congregation) to the services with what the individual can perform (without creating discrimination between services: big, small, male, or female) and encourage them to serve. They should have a well-organised way (policy) of delineating and using wisely by deploying and providing the necessary training expected from the church leaders. They must mentor those assigned if they are not serving the church correctly by looking into their problems and giving them the training to enable them to do their work if they lack any skill and knowledge to accomplish their assignment.

Service for the Lord shall not be assigned to someone frowning, they should not need to be begged, not given to sluggish, not at all. No one should act in such a way since the Lord will be watching from the heavens. Because God never accepts a sacrifice that has ill blemish.

"And if there be any blemish therein, as if it be lame, blind, or have any ill defect, thou shalt not sacrifice it unto the Lord thy God." (Deuteronomy 15:21)

Therefore, we shall be careful not to bring any sacrifice that has any blemish. We shall give our service with the anointing that we are gifted with in full for the glory of God.

Hence, nobody shall remain short of giving the best of his service and must show more significant effort to excel. Unfortunately, currently, due to work and different engagements, people seem to be busy and don't have spare leisure time and thus don't have time to give service to the Lord by attending church services and assignments. Therefore only a few are observed giving time to serve. This situation must change. Every person should serve God for his own sake in any field he can perform.

You must serve God. When God created every human being on this earth, He gave everyone a unique talent/ gift. Some animals run; some swim; some dig holes; some jump; some fly with their wings. As per the character, He made each the way they act accordingly. Some of us know to perform something specifically, we are made to do so.

According to my thinking, I believe that the church has a significant population spread worldwide. Each Sunday, the benches are filled with people who come to worship God to 'protect' their faith, but do nothing.

Most messages focus on saying 'awaken' to church members, meaning Christians who regularly come to church to support the church financially. It seems to mean nothing more vital to them than giving money. But God desires more than this. Each Christian should exercise the gift he gives to the service of God without reservation. If the local church can make use of all the anointing God gave to His people, something miraculous can happen.

13. ARE WE READY TO PAY THE SACRIFICE THAT THE SERVICE REQUIRES?

Serving God may require you to pay sacrifice. We see this written in the Word of God in many places. When King David was about to present his sacrifice, he had to buy the site from Araunah even if he tried to offer him free of charge; David refused to take it for free-thinking; he had to pay the price for it. Let us see what it says in the following verse:

"And the king said unto Araunah, Nay; but I will surely buy it of thee at a price: neither will I offer burnt offerings unto the Lord my God of that which doth cost me nothing. So David bought the threshing floor and the oxen for fifty shekels of silver." (2 Samuel 24:24)

When we say we want to serve God, we have to sacrifice our time, energy, money, or anything we have for the service that is needed, and any sacrifice to provide the service. Isn't all that is given to us from Him? So, from what He gave us, why not offer the little we can since He is the one who will replace it? Why, then, shall we try to surrender without weighing its value? We need to correct and walk correcting ourselves and try to serve Him with all we have, not unless we are ignorant or knowingly make mistakes from our fleshly weakness.

Focusing on the flesh needs to fulfil all its needs; even when we lack time, we try to compromise and meet its demand. Do we make sure that we attempt to serve the Lord to do more to fulfil His purpose? Knowing and doing this is very important.

From this point of view, we observe most of the time when the church calls for fasting and prayer when there is an all-night prayer program, not many participate. Why should this be? No one is absent when there is an invitation to attend a wedding ceremony; why then, when the service issue comes in the house of God, why are people not coming in their numbers? What is the problem? Which one is more important?

"And say to Archippus, Take heed to the ministry which thou hast received in the Lord, that thou fulfill it." (Colossians 4:17)

As we are spiritual people, instead of seeking a lot of pleasure and fleshly joy, we should be looking for something that will make God happy and give us better rewards as Christians. Therefore, we should make more effort to provide Him exemplary service at the right time and place.

14. WHAT SHALL WE DO TO THOSE WHO DO NOT BELIEVE THE GOSPEL?

As we all understand, the number of people dying, particularly in Africa and Ethiopia, is increasing. Studies show that people die due to internal conflict, transmissible diseases, hunger, drought, and car accidents, which are the main reasons to perish. If we check how many of them could have received Jesus out of these people, we could probably find one percent.

As we all understand, the Bible tells us precisely that he will be going to eternal death unless he accepts Jesus Christ as his medicine, as his personal Lord and God.

Churches worldwide have a responsibility and vision of spreading the gospel to those who haven't heard it. People, or in Greek, *ethne,* have primary foundational space in the New Testament. He has a plan to save the children of God. In the Old Testament and when we read the gospel messages, mainly when we look into the book of Revelations, we notice that disciples can be from any people in the world. Therefore, we have to pray for the church to reach this goal! So that it can have a strategic approach and methods. However, the idea of *ethne* is that the church must understand it well. This idea should be part of it.

Most of the world's population do not know Christ, live in a different religion or faith, are devoid of the truth, and are in the darkness.

Not knowing is the responsibility of the gospel believers to bring these people to the light and preach the gospel.

All of us came to accept Jesus after being preached the gospel one way or the other, telling us about the saving power of Jesus.

"For whosoever shall call upon the name of the Lord shall be saved. How then shall they call on him in whom they have not believed? and how shall they believe in him of whom they have not heard? and how shall they hear without a preacher? And how shall they preach, except they are sent? as it is written, how beautiful are the feet of them that preach the Gospel of peace, and bring glad tidings of good things!" (Roman 10:13-15)

All gospel believers must work hard to spread the gospel to those who have not heard; you must make a profit with the talent you have taken, whether small or big, you must multiply it. To perform this, we need not ask permission from church leaders. Witnessing the gospel is given to every believer; therefore, we have to make more profit with spiritual envy and effort.

Of course, service requires knowledge and technical know-how of how to do it; thus, you need to be skilled. Regarding training, leaders must give a well-designed, organised workshop to those who want to work in this line, select those with gifts and anointing, and assign them to do the job.

When the church gives you service, you must perform with great determination and try to invite souls to the house of the Lord and register successful results. Service is a responsibility we received from Jesus the first time we accepted Him; therefore, we should not ignore it.

Snatching people living in the dark is something even the angels in the heavens rejoice with psalms and songs more than anything.

"I say unto you, that likewise, joy shall be in heaven over one sinner that repenteth, more than over ninety and nine just persons, which need no repentance." (Luke 15:7)

We must also work on our talent and present the souls we can save to Him. Only then shall we expect to have more glory before the Lord.

CHAPTER 2

15. LET US EXAMINE OUR RELATIONSHIP WITH JESUS

Jesus Christ has told us that the world knows we are His disciples when we love each other.

Jesus called the disciples to Him from where they were living, and made them followers when He knew it was nearing His time of ascension. His instruction to the disciples was to follow in the future and practice what He taught. This instruction was the law of love; to love each other and practice this. When they do this, people will know they are the disciples of Jesus from their actions; they will realise they belong to Jesus. When they love each other, they will witness that they have changed, and Jesus is living among them. John tells us in his message in 1 John 3:4 that it means that one who doesn't have love will be walking in darkness in the evening.

The Jews separated themselves from those living in a particular place known as Kumaran. They were called Mennonites. No one told them to love each other and showed them love in practice. They were known as 'Children of light', and others were known as 'Children of the Darkness'. The church leaders did not preach Jesus' love to anyone who said, "As much as I love you, you must love each other." No one showed them the way out. But Jesus's teaching was of the type of love He gave us "This is my commandment, That ye love one another, as I have loved you. Greater love hath no man than this, that a man lay down his life for his friends" (as it says in John 15:12-13).

As we are human beings, what do we feel when we meet with people on this planet? How do we feel when we meet at times of what we do, the ideas we share, the life we share through marriage, the meals we share, in times of mourning and joy? What does it look like? We need to check ourselves on these and other concerning issues.

It is common practice for people to visit friends and bring a gift as a gesture of thanks. Because of this, they become close to each other, and their friendship strengthens. What becomes a problem is if there is no exchange of benefits; how do we treat someone who doesn't give any use, like any ordinary person in a marketplace, or a worship place. Let us look back for a while how we treat people.

God wants us to develop our relationship through cooperation and love. Whenever there is division and disagreement as Christians, the name of our Lord will be tarnished when we are with family or meet with a Christian fellow, this means we are His church. Is our relationship with others based on love and unity or separation and division? Do we love our children, encourage them, or always think of ourselves? Do we focus more on ourselves enjoying our living situations than others?

We might think we have absolute righteousness from our brothers and sisters; do we feel bad if we don't find them as expected? We need to love people together with their mistakes and weaknesses. If we don't approach them in this manner, we become police or judges.

One of the main commandments the Lord gave us is the one that says, "love your friend as yourself." Therefore, to be obedient is not done by calculating advantage or when it is convenient, but by practicing it without setting any criteria.

"And the second is like, namely this, thou shalt love thy neighbor as thyself. There are none other commandments more significant than these." (Mark 12:31)

Apart from this, the direction we choose to go might mean we lose and not profit in life. Therefore, to celebrate the Lord in life, we should force ourselves to respect His commandments.

If this is the situation before us, we shall practice it for our benefit without anyone forcing us. The Lord can examine our kidneys and heart, thus let us respond to ourselves honestly (Psalm 7:9).

When our relationship with God breaks, it will not be corrected just because we do it anyway; similarly, when our relationship with people is damaged, it will not help us restore our relationship with God.

Let us check ourselves against the following questions:

16. WHO IS YOUR FRIEND?

"And, behold, a particular lawyer stood up, and tempted him, saying Master, what shall I do to inherit eternal life? He said unto him, what is written in the law? How readest thou? And he answering said Thou shalt love the Lord thy God with all thy heart, and with all thy soul, and with all thy strength, and with all thy mind; and thy neighbor as thyself. And he answering said Thou shalt love the Lord thy God with all thy heart, and with all thy soul, and with all thy strength, and with all thy mind; and thy neighbor as thyself. And he said unto him, thou hast answered right: this do, and thou shalt live. But he, willing to justify himself, said unto Jesus, And who is my neighbor? And Jesus answering said, A confident man went down from Jerusalem to Jericho, fell among thieves, stripped him of his raiment, wounded him, and departed, leaving him half dead. And by chance there came down a certain priest that way: and when he saw him, he passed by on the other side. And likewise a Levite, when he was at the place, came and looked on him, and passed by on the other side. But a certain Samaritan, as he journeyed, came where he was: and when he saw him, he had compassion on him, And went to him, and bound up his wounds, pouring in oil and wine, and set him on his own beast, and brought him to an inn, and took care of him. And on the morrow when he departed, he took out two pence, and gave them to the host, and said unto him, take care of him; and whatsoever thou spendest more, when I come again, I will repay thee. Which now of these three, thinkest thou, was neighbor unto him that fell among the thieves? And he said, He that showed mercy on him. Then said Jesus unto him, Go, and do thou likewise." (Luke 10:25-37)

In our society, a friend means growing up together, a close friend, a peer group, or because of different circumstances introduced and eventually knowing each other and connecting for some time are to be friends.

The Lord's teachings are not the same as those of a friend or brother of this type. But, still, as to Him, he means to make every man or woman created in the image and likeness of God on this earth, regardless of ethnicity, colour, religion, or nationality, be a friend to us that we see them moving on this earth.

From this point of view, what would be our response? Do we consider every human being as our friend? Or do we entertain friends who are the nearest ones we have been dealing with that will benefit us? But what we need to know and do is the word written to us correctly. If we attach ourselves to the ones close to us and shy away from those not close to us, it means His commandment did not work on us. Therefore, we shall understand what needs to correct and live correctly according to the Word.

The law teacher (as we find in Matthew 12:31) raised a question that says, "love your friend like yourself." If you find it anywhere, then why do you want to be excused for not doing it? The law teacher's view of the commandment of Jesus should not be felt as there is a good excuse to not do it. He questioned again, saying, "I don't have a friend; how will I implement what you said?" In the eyes of the law teacher, a friend means a peer who does something in return for what you have done to him. A friend means, as people mostly understand, one who will return by doing good because of the mutual friendship you develop when you do them good. To the law teacher, a friend is spiritually clean like him. To the law teacher, a friend gives and takes mutual benefits.

The law teacher considers his friend who will invite you when you ask him, gives gifts when you give him gifts, and does well when you do good to him. The law teacher, in spiritual terms, does something equivalent to what you did and is a righteous person.

In the eyes of the law teacher, he makes friends by looking at his peer group and exchanging benefits equally. But in the eyes of Jesus, a friend is created by doing something good to human beings. If you want to make a friend, be good to someone. To find a friend, you must do something good for someone. It would help if you did not wait for someone to be good to you to see a friend. If you want a friend, do good. You are a friend to the one you have been good to. Anybody you have been good to is your wealth. Those you have been good to are your jewels. Those you were good to are for your glory. If you want to multiply your friends, then multiply by doing good. You are a friend to all you were good to, in particular to those you have done well, and a forefront celebrity to those you have done especially well. You are wealthy to those you have done charity. There is nobody more than you who is a remedy to those you have done well.

"Which now of these three, thinkest thou, was neighbour unto him that fell among the thieves? And he said, He that showed mercy on him. Then said Jesus unto him, Go, and do thou likewise." (Luke 10:36-37)

17. DO WE LOVE OUR FRIENDS AS OURSELVES?

No one in the world doesn't love himself. Therefore, it is not a sin to love oneself. However, the Lord commands us that much as we love ourselves, we shall also love our friends. Is this possible or not? I think it is better if each person shall answer this question. But respecting and keeping His Word is a guarantee and has no other option for us.

The Word tells us God is love; hence, if God Himself is love and we say we know Him and appear in His image and likeness, His love must live in us. If His love dwells in us, it must be visible. It will be displayed when we love others in the love that He loved us with. In this way, if we can't love, we don't know God.

"He that loveth not knoweth not God; for God is love." (1 John 4:8)

18. DO WE APPROACH OUR FRIENDS WITH THE STEADFAST LOVE OF THE LORD?

What does true love mean? How do we display it? We can raise these and many other similar questions. To us weak and sinful, Jesus revealed His Love by going up to the calvary on the Cross. Will there be anyone among us that will express their love in such a manner?

"For scarcely for a righteous man will one die: yet peradventure for a good man some would even dare to die." (Romans 5:7)

To greet each other once a week by rubbing shoulders when we meet on Sundays, or shaking hands to salute, or say "Hi" with words does not show the level of love we have for each other. Because the love in us through Christ is so high, on our part, the minimum expected is that we shall try to accept each other, be concerned about each other, cooperate, and agree with each other. In this regard, does this show the love we offer to people? If not, we shall diligently work to have that type of love.

"Though I speak with the tongues of men and of angels, and have not charity, I am become as sounding brass, or a tinkling cymbal. And though I have the gift of prophecy, and understand all mysteries, and all knowledge; and though I have all faith, so that I could remove mountains, and have not charity, I am nothing. And though I bestow all my goods to feed the poor, and though I give my body to be burned, and have not charity, it profiteth me nothing." (1 Corinthians 13:1-3)

The message presented above is deep and robust and cannot be real, not unless we try make it happen in our lives. We shall try hard to hold on to what is advantageous and make our value respected and a precious gem before the Lord. Let us check ourselves with the questions listed below and examine and try to correct and fulfil them.

19. FOR A RELATIONSHIP, DO WE TAKE EVERYONE AS HE IS?

Man, by nature, prefers to be closer to those who benefit him and distance from those who distance him. Such closeness is fleshly, but we know we must love every human being as God tells us. But are we able to love any person we find next to us? Having such love is where the issue is. If all people could love any person next to them according to the Word, then generally, there wouldn't be a problem of quarrelling and disagreement. In the world wars and killing each other, dividing into different groups would have been avoided, the world could have been a better place of peace and stability, and we would have loved everyone. Peaceful co-existence became a problem from the time of Abel and Cain; hatred and contradiction between people started as early as that time. The fight and violent actions between people resulted in hatred. Do we greet each other when we meet someone face to face, or only call them on the phone?

Do we pray to our brother or sister as much as the Holy Spirit reminds us?

If we see in our brother or sister a mistake/error, do we try to become closer and correct, advise politely, and return with love, humility, and encouragement? Or are we judging to show ourselves we stand for the glory of the Lord and condemn the person perishing millions of lives in the years past; it even continues, as we can see now. Despite such situations, the world is going on without peace. Although the Lord of peace, Jesus Christ, paid the price for peace and was resurrected by His Father more than two thousand years ago, the world is still without peace and did not reconcile as taught by the Lord of peace.

As we all know, the level of peace depends on reason when we come closer to people. But Jesus never looked for preconditions or reasons to receive us when He drew us to Him. So why do we have a problem if this is what He taught us in His gospel?

"Beloved, let us love one another: for love is of God, and everyone that loveth is born of God and knoweth God. He that loveth not knoweth not God; for God is love. In this was manifested the love of God toward us, because that God sent his only begotten Son into the world, that we might live through him. Herein is love, not that we loved God, but that he loved us, and sent his Son to be the propitiation for our sins. Beloved, if God so loved us, we ought also to love one another. No man hath seen God at any time. If we love one another, God dwelleth in us, and his love is perfected in us." (John 4:7-12)

As we see in many places, those who believe and are saved in Jesus Christ have their connection differently. Therefore, we shall try to answer and analyse the situation and examine how it looks from the points mentioned hereunder.

Without sympathising, let us check why.

- Do we accept our brother or sister as better than us, or do we neglect them?
- Do we happily accept our brother or sister with their weaknesses?

- If we have a different view over a particular faith, do we try to share and learn from each other, humbly and patiently?
- Do we try to make our friendship based on God's Word with our brethren and sisters?

We can raise these and other issues of concern by putting on the correct measurements and checking what we are missing to correct them.

Lord Jesus loved us enough to give up His own life with what is known as "agape" love, which means it doesn't count any error, and we are so weak that we can't give as much love as He did, but we need to love people from the whole heart as much as we can practically. In this, to practice in our life, grace is there to help us. For this, the Word tells us we have the heart of Christ. "For who hath known the mind of the Lord, that he may instruct him? But we have the mind of Christ" (Corinthians 2:16).

We have the heart of Christ, which means we have the love, charity, sympathy, and forgiveness that makes us love just like Christ has. If this is the case, why do we see in churches around us that there is hatred, separation, quarrel, argument, misunderstanding, rejection, and anger? Will it always be there? There could be many reasons for this. However, this indicates that we are not obeying His words and shows these problems in our lives.

None of us can have any reason not to love anyone except for our sinfulness. God has loved us without cause; we must love all human beings. Therefore, we shall not be close to some with reason and distance from others.

Without loving those next to us, we are liars if we say we love God.

"He that loveth not knoweth not God; for God is love." (1 John 4:8)

"And we have known and believed the love that God hath to us. God is love; and he that dwelleth in love dwelleth in God, and God in him." (1 John 4:16)

It doesn't need any additional explanation. Therefore, whoever says he knows God should have love (that loves everyone). But, to love a human being, you cannot set criteria to say 'I like this one and hate the other.' If we do so, it will be like not knowing the Word because there are no criteria written as unique identification to say it should be this type of person you should love.

If love exists among people, then great things can happen. Love in the book of Corinthians is listed as follows:

"Though I speak with the tongues of men and of angels, and have not charity, I am become as sounding brass, or a tinkling cymbal. And though I have the gift of prophecy, and understand all mysteries, and all knowledge; and though I have all faith so that I could remove mountains, and have not charity, I am nothing. And though I bestow all my goods to feed the poor, and though I give my body to be burned, and have not charity, it profiteth me nothing. Charity suffereth long and is kind; charity envieth not; charity vaunteth, not itself, is not puffed up, Doth not behave itself unseemly, seeketh not her own, is not easily provoked, thinketh no evil; Rejoiceth not in iniquity, but rejoiceth in the truth; Beareth all things, believeth all things, hopeth all things, endureth all things. Charity never faileth: but whether there be prophecies, they shall fail; whether there be tongues, they shall cease; whether there be knowledge, it shall vanish away." (Corinthians 13:1-8)

Whatever we do will not be good unless we do it in love. It doesn't matter how well we do as far as we don't have love; it is useless without love. So, our love for each other shows that we are disciples of Jesus Christ.

CHAPTER 3

20. LET US CHECK OUR RELATIONSHIPS

How shall we meet each other?

As Christians, how should our relationships be? It is a fundamental question. As human beings, we meet with people in the family or outsiders (other people). We know that friends, family, society, and international relations exist among humans. These relations have got their purpose. But, of course, the people of God also participate in any ordinary way. However, when Christians have a relationship, there are some things they will be doing.

Our relationship will be healthy and smooth, mainly depending on the family or church relationships we have during our life. When the tiny finger is hurt, the whole body feels the pain. Similarly, God has told us the same way we may feel uncomfortable in our social relationships when something goes wrong in our relationship. Because of this, we can't stay in harmony, and our peaceful co-existence can be complex.

"If it be possible, as much as lieth in you, live peaceably with all men." (Romans 12:18)

"Follow peace with all men, and holiness, without which no man shall see the Lord." (Hebrews 12:14)

The Word tells us that if we can't live with other people in peace, we can't see the Lord. So, we must ask ourselves, "If we do not live a life in peace with people that can make us see the Lord, then what would benefit our Christianity?" Because our primary goal is to see the Lord, to be with Him. Anything other than this, whatever we use for glory, wealth, pride, prosperity, joy, and success, is all for our flesh but not for spiritual benefit. Thus, it doesn't have any use. One thing that makes God happy is our love for each other. Is there any reason to make God unhappy? Who helped us live with His blessings and protection? Indeed, with every human being in behaviour, feeling, thinking, preference, we are different, and we may not agree on everything. God who created us knows very well that He made us all unique, but when He said to love each other, He knew some conditions would give us comfort or otherwise we will have difficulties with each other.

What choice do we have except to follow what we must do when we try to make criteria? Which man can be knowledgeable of God? We need, therefore, to use His words by checking which one does agree or does not agree with the Word. Hence, our relationship must be as peaceful as possible. Being peace creators, we must know our obligation and sacrifice to have such a situation with everyone. The Word strengthens by saying in "If it be possible, as much as lieth in you, live peaceably with all men." (Romans 12:18)

Let us see some of the points according to the Word of God to check ourselves from the following:

Loving each other

Above all, the first commandment is to love your God, and the second says to love your neighbours/friends.

"And thou shalt love the Lord thy God with all thy heart, and with all thy soul, and with all thy mind, and with all thy strength: this is the first commandment. And the second is like, namely this, Thou shalt love thy neighbor as thyself. There are none other commandments more significant than these." (Mark 12:30-31)

"For all the law is fulfilled in one word, even in this." (Galatians 5:14)

Thou shalt love thy neighbour as thyself.

Liking or loving in terms of the spiritual translation does not give the same meaning as the relation between female and male intimacy. This connection is to the one taught by Christ Jesus and how He loved all human beings. Such love among Christians must grow, and above all, our passion should include loving others.

It can be challenging for those outside the church and those who do not know the Lord. We are the ones who should come close and witness Him. If we cannot love them, we cannot preach the gospel to them, and nothing will force us to do so. Even with those who have received the Lord, we cannot practice what we have to if we do not love each other. We cannot worship together, serve, fulfil His will, and respect the laws. Because of this situation, we must be careful because we can only see the Lord if we develop the pure intent of love for each other and take care not to fall short of it.

Indeed, the type of love Lord Jesus loved us with is called agape; with no critics, He went to the extent of giving His own life with extraordinary love. Although we are human beings, we cannot display that type of love as much as He did; if we full-heartedly take it up, we should be able to show love like Him. For us to love, His grace will help us reveal it in our lives. To be able to do this, we have the heart of Jesus as the Word says.

"For who knows the mind of the Lord, that he may instruct him? But we have the mind of Christ." (1 Corinthians 2:16)

Having the heart of Christ means his love, humility, blessing, sympathy, mercifulness, etc., just like Christ did, which He has given us through His Spirit. If this is the case, as we have observed many times in the church, why do people have hatred, quarrel, argument, misunderstanding, contempt, etc.? There could be many reasons for this, but mainly why we are not keeping our relationship in love is the problem emanating from not watching His Word and not practicing.

We cannot love someone because we are not living in His words. God has loved us all without any condition; we also are expected to love every human unconditionally. Therefore, we cannot distance ourselves from any human for a reason we make.

"He that loveth not knoweth not God; for God is love." (1 John 4:8)

"And we have known and believed the love that God hath to us. God is love; and he that dwelleth in love dwelleth in God, and God in him." (1 John 4:16)

We don't need any other explanation for this. Thus, whoever says I know God must love every human being (which allows him to love all). Therefore, it must be someone who doesn't know the Word who sets a criterion to love someone if someone says, 'I love someone because of this criterion or hate another one because of that criterion.' It doesn't work because no standard exists for love or hate.

Many great things happen when there is love among people. It is explained in the Word as follows:

"Though I speak with the tongues of men and of angels, and have not charity, I am become as sounding brass, or a tinkling cymbal. And though I have the gift of prophecy, and understand all mysteries, and all knowledge; and though I have all faith, so that I could remove mountains, and have not charity, I am nothing. And though I bestow all my goods to feed the poor, and though I give my body to be burned, and have not charity, it profiteth me nothing. Charity suffereth long and is kind; charity envieth not; charity vaunteth, not itself, is not puffed up, Doth not behave itself unseemly, seeketh not her own, is not easily provoked, thinketh no evil; Rejoiceth not in iniquity, but rejoiceth in the truth; Beareth all things, believeth all things, hopeth all things, endureth all things. Charity never faileth: but whether there be prophecies, they shall fail; whether there be tongues, they shall cease; whether there be knowledge, it shall vanish away." (1 Corinthians 13:1-8)

Unless we do it with true love, it doesn't matter how much work we do; it will be useless. As far as love is not there, it will show valuelessness openly. The love we have for each other is a way that will show that we are disciples of Christ.

Accepting each other

Accepting is essential to living together, serving, worshipping, participating, agreeing on an idea, etc. The reason we discuss acceptance is because there is the problem of not receiving each other. Christ loved us without waiting for us to accept Him. He took us as we are, and we should make ourselves and other people the same way. One of the issues that develops internal problems is the lack of acknowledgment of the status of each other. Everyone accepts himself but fails to take another person. He forgives himself but wants to judge another person. He tries to grow slowly for himself but loses hope in the slow development of others.

It tells us that the church's unity of Romans was disturbed because of not accepting, as explained in this book. Not taking each other with love created two factions that previously worshipped only one Lord and ended up divided. If they were worshipping one Lord, the congregation should have remained one. Instead, they tried to make their disagreement spiritual for their division. One of them lost their love thinking he was the only one who understood. The others thought their envy was of God's house and started condemning them.

Some considered themselves God's closest helper, a revealer of the veil. So, when they didn't take it, they were full of contempt and judgement in the church. If the honourable believer in the Lord despises another, God will be disappointed if one doesn't mercifully judge the other.

One who thinks he is knowledgeable should make clear his capacity with love. He should worship Christ, not his liberty. When we say one who understands the truth, we mean not he has a conscience but that the Holy Spirit has governed him. The fact he respects today means he had been opposing it yesterday. He should think God did not shut the door after taking in others. God has a purpose for the weak individual; we should believe He is the father to all. The tarnisher and condemner shall not consider it as if it is his command and be disappointed. Instead, I should think about how I can leave behind my brother and believe lovingly about others. Christianity that doesn't have love is dead. Service without love does not glorify God. He was born in the manger because He wanted to save, but He could have judged from His throne if Christ wanted.

We need to accept each other. We need the arms of the Holy Spirit while we get each other's ideas with the right mind to use them for our good.

Our creation is to be different from one another, even with fingerprints and special eye characters; similarly, our design is different in our behaviour. But this is not supposed to be a reason for not accepting, and it should be taken as our beauty to understand each other and create a conducive situation to help each other.

We know that we have differences of opinion, and the critical point we need to consider is using this opportunity to filter out the best workable situation from the worst that may not work well. So, please choose the one that can bring us together, avoid the one we did not agree on after discussing the options, leave out the one we did not agree on, and then implement what we agreed on.

The one whose idea is the best should not boast, and the one whose idea did not win should not be disappointed; it is essential to be ready to work together. This problem is not common in religious organisations, but it is prevalent in political organisations where politicians argue visibly. This situation goes into hatred for each other and may even go to the extent of individual assassination, war, etc., history books tell us this. But we are given the heart of Christ, and the commandment says we should love each other, thus, we cannot enter into such contradiction or struggle.

Some people are rigid, they do not accept other people's opinions even if the idea is much better than theirs. On the other hand, they may not have any critical ideas but rather criticise others with no valuable ideas, and they like opposing them. Some people think they know and are wise, neglect other people's opinions, and tend not to accept others' ideas. People fail to tolerate and move to separation when such a situation happens. Taking the house of God like a human house and separating it is a colossal mistake. First, it violates the commandment that says, "if you can live in peace with every human being"; secondly, it will be a big mistake to depart from the house of the Lord just by disagreeing with some people. Separation is like sin.

"Now the works of the flesh are manifest, which are these; Adultery, fornication, uncleanness, lasciviousness, idolatry, witchcraft, hatred, variance, emulations, wrath, strife, seditions, heresies, envying, murders, drunkenness, revelling, and such like: of the which I tell you before, as I have also told you in time past, that they which do such things shall not inherit the kingdom of God." (Galatians 5:19-21)

In Galatians, one of the things mentioned in the work of the flesh is separation. Separation is a problem that comes from not having acceptance for each other.

For this, the best typical solution should investigate the source of the problem for the people affected. The affected people must open their hearts to solve their problems by broadening their shoulders to agree to sit around a table and discuss. Then listen to each other's opinions, select what they think is better, and wind up on that. Delay discussion on points they haven't agreed on to keep their unity healthy and continue some other time. They will develop the Christian image, accept each other, and know this through their life and behavioural reflection when they can do this.

Acceptance involves knowing each other, respecting others, considering social relations, etc., and expecting effective results. However, this does not mean that changes through time should not be permanent without making changes.

Man's behaviour is variable. The Lord is the only one that doesn't change and is valid. If we can control our thinking, human beings can continue without changing our behaviour. We must notice and return if a problem can take us out of our way. God created a big brain that does this. We must use this big brain adequately and put it to practice.

We can decide if we should discuss whatever level of problem we have. Suppose people are not debating openly over an issue, leave the church alone, institutions, etc. In that case, husband and wife could not have peace, which would not continue peacefully. Chances are slim to agree on a common point.

If couples are not praying together on disappointments or disagreements, their marriage will be in danger. For such solutions, the discussion is the solution. Discussing together with goodwill will bring a result that God likes. The important thing is to gain a life that will make God happy; we should pay any sacrifice to make Him happy. Any Christian who doesn't want to do this must think because it will be a fruitless effort.

Agreeing with one another

Because of the one Spirit we shared, the things that make us agree, be together, have one heart, and more importantly, the idea that separates or makes us different from the rest of the world for gospel believers is our jewel.

Agreeing on something can be taken as interconnection and goes within contrast or familiarity. The agreement requires one idea and not looking for differences to decide on /an idea that needs attention in one vote. The Holy Spirit dislikes separation and this one Spirit works in all and does not like separation.

"For the Lord, the God of Israel, saith that he hateth putting away: for one covereth violence with his garment, saith the Lord of hosts: therefore take heed to your spirit, that ye deal not treacherously." (Malachi 2:16)

"And let none of you imagine evil in your hearts against his neighbor; and love no false oath: for all these are things that I hate, saith the Lord." (Zechariah 8:17)

As the above verse explains, God has told us the issue He doesn't want to see in our lives. If we ignore this and go on our will and do what we want to, try to worship Him, we will draw disaster or destruction on ourselves.

"Agree with thin adversary quickly, whiles thou art in the way with him; lest the adversary deliver thee to the judge, and the judge deliver thee to the officer, and thou be cast into prison." (Mathew 5:25)

Two servants of God served in one church because they could not have peace; one had to be transferred to a far-away church and get helped there. The church leaders thought that instead of the servants separating because of their disagreement, they should organise a dinner and make them reconcile, and thus, prepared a dinner invitation program. On the day of the invitation, organisers gave the chance to make a speech to the outgoing person. Therefore, he shared the phrase from Luke 15:22: "You remain with the donkey, my son and I will go there to worship and return to you." The individual spoke sarcastically, saying, "The one staying with you is the donkey," and they understood. Unfortunately, the reconciliation didn't happen, and it ended without achieving its objectives as planned.

Holding anger and sleeping with it will be a reason for resentment. Therefore, whoever loves the Lord and serves Him, shall not be angry at his brother and sleep. As the Lord Jesus said, "When you approach God for a prayer or gift, if you have some disappointment with your brother, give priority to go and ask forgiveness from your brother before you kneel to pray, then you come and continue your prayer" (Matthew 5:23-24), this is what He taught us. If one cannot do this, according to the commandment of the Lord, it may not be well, his sacrifice may not be ascending, his gift is not received, and he becomes helpless.

That is why our forefathers, who understood that resentment and prayer can never go together, said in the proverbs: "Praying while having irritation is just like 'trying to steal while having a cough.'"

As Christians, we should talk and agree on whatever disappointment we face.

"Can two walk together, except they are agreed?" (Amos 3:3)

Edifying each other

Like any other social life in our relationships, there must be evident support for each additional and spiritual support. It is necessary to be developed as Christians to enlighten, encourage, and make the excellent work continue, creating a solid effort for each other must be the reliable and exemplary work we need.

Indeed, among Africans, edifying is not our culture that sets a tremendous impact. Still, as Christians, to shape our newborns, we shall be free from this backward culture and come out praising each other and encouraging, thereby developing this practice.

We shall make this a heritage inheritance by changing ourselves and passing it on to our children. Whether the performed activity is minor or significant, we look at whether it happened with the right or wrong intention for the house of God and if it benefits those who rest under it. If achieved, the one who did this, brother, or sister, must be thanked, encouraged, and even assist the individual in performing better, bright ideas. Improving ideas will have to be given to impact an outstanding contribution.

After changing ourselves, we shall teach and hand over the good things we have practiced to our children. Whatever is going on, whether small or big, the important thing is that they work for the house of God, and the duty must be with an upright, willing heart, and those who rest under it should be helpful. Then, we shall encourage the person to do more and give ideas to make the person do more productive things; this requires making the person close and improving relations and has an outstanding contribution.

"Let no corrupt communication proceed out of your mouth, but that which is good to the use of edifying, that it may minister grace unto the hearers." (Ephesians 4:29)

"How is it then, brethren? when ye come together, every one of you hath a psalm, hath a doctrine, hath a tongue, hath a revelation, hath an interpretation. Let all things be done unto edifying." (1 Corinthians 14:26)

In any respect, our edification for each other must come from positive feelings. The choice is only one, i.e., to the person we want to encourage, we shall do it with a good sense and positivity.

People can encourage each other in different ways. But the main thing is that we shall have a loving heart. Constructive edification is giving positive remarks to improve a person for what he has done or trying to constructively bring the idea, which is a sacred idea. Therefore, when service people stand on the pulpit to deliver a service and call upon or glorify the name of the Lord our God and bless the title, we should loudly respond with "Amen!" without reservation. Amen simultaneously encourages the service members and trembles the enemy and contributes to bringing glory to God. Because of this, the congregants must be diligent to say amen loud enough.

Not only when we meet in God's house, but it must also be a practice to give constructive edifying comments when someone is doing something important at any time and place to encourage the person to continue. Therefore, it is appropriate for any Christian to apply carefully. The congregation should encourage a person in the church for his service. The assembly must appropriately applaud, without exaggerating, to encourage him to be built up in his service to God.

Giving servants unnecessary respect and praise they don't deserve might lead them to count themselves equal to the Lord and consider themselves clean, forgetting their weaknesses. Inappropriate recognition may lead them to temptation and invite them to lose direction from God. Unnecessary credit might take them to divert from the right track. There is a need for thought and understanding, for an enslaved person is not greater than his master. The Lord Jesus himself told his disciples "The disciple is not above his master, nor the servant above his lord." (Matthew 10:24)

It's going to be nice when everything is done correctly and in the right way. There it is possible to serve the will of God. To upbuild, we need to share the blessings, and the main point is to encourage one another and focus on helping him be strong in spirit and action. The criticism highlights the error, which can be counterproductive if not handled carefully. However, what should happen is to emphasise the solid and good deed first and make the criticism second so that it builds up and can express and correct the person constructively and instructively. He is doing what is wrong because he is working, for if he was not working, what opportunity is there for him to err? Let us, therefore, make a change of heart in this regard, that we may reap what we sow, for the benefits are for all of us.

Helping each other

To do the work of the house of God, we need to help each other. The result can be cumbersome unless we combine our energy, knowledge, time, finance, and material. It becomes challenging and causes the problem. Since the work is extensive and sometimes complex, it can be challenging to see it not being accomplished if the church doesn't get our cooperation to work together compellingly. If we don't move by gathering our knowledge, time, money, and materials to help the work, there might be challenges to do the job. If there is no coordinated effort to do the work and it cannot get the required help from members, difficult work situations can often occur. To help each other, we need to have a good conscience, goodwill, accept each other, and walk in love; it is a must. Church leaders and ministers creating this situation should play an early role and be a sound and practical example. The source of church progress: leadership qualifications and the people should focus on the leadership's admission of willingness to work and travel together.

What needs to be noticed here is that there should be a healthy relationship between church leaders and the people of God because God ordains church leaders and ministers. It should be a spiritual relationship, not a relationship between boss and servant, but a father and daughter, a brother and sister, and a relationship of respect and acceptance. So, leaders and ministers are considered like equal fellows to each other.

Since responsibility is not easy, it is the work of the house of God, so everyone in the house of God should be a fellow worker and a contributor to the responsibilities to one designated by church leaders and work on that in the spirit of solidarity and love. It's hard to imagine how God, who loved our union, would want to show us His glory among us as we line up in His house and do the work of the house. Therefore, we need to be fully aware that the reason for seeking unity at home is not for anyone's benefit but first for our good.

Sometimes there's a chance that people will be obedient to someone they love and disobey someone they don't like. This kind of thinking shouldn't work in the house of God. We shouldn't associate the work we do in His place with anyone. We ought to understand it is for the glory of our God and vested interests. And no matter what problems or obstacles we may face at work, we must continue to do as much as possible to ensure we do the job. As Nehemiah trusted in God, who sustained us by his undeserved kindness, we should not investigate our hardships.

"The God of heaven, he will prosper us; therefore, we his servants will arise and build." (Nehemiah 2:20)

We notice that the differences of opinion often observed between people influenced and hindered the work of God's house. We must note that such an obstacle can always be from the enemy. If anyone interferes with the doing of good in the house of Yahweh in any way, let him examine himself. If something outside the world happens, that need must stop. Moreover, the work must reflect on helping and accomplishing with a sincere spirit. If there is a significant breach of the word and confidence in the planned work, it is right to inform and urge church leaders and ministers to resolve the issue according to the dish before protesting. However, it would be wrong to oppose and cause or hinder an uproar without that. Because problems can sometimes arise from a lack of understanding or detail, ensuring and trying to understand the pre-planned situation and its fulfilment can save it from mass resistance and obstruction. In this way, emotions in people distinguish between the parishioners and the leaders of God's house and prevent work from taking place. Everyone must be diligently protected, so this doesn't happen in the house of God.

In addition to helping in church activities, the people of God's house need to cooperate and help in the context of the social crisis. People's earthly life is not the same, and they are known to live in the upper, middle, and lower classes. Since each person lives according to their diligence and abilities, it is appropriate and biblical to recognise this and support and assist those facing life's problems in the best and most convenient way possible.

"Well reported of for good works; if she has brought up children, if she has lodged strangers, if she has washed the saints' feet, if she has relieved the afflicted, if she has diligently followed every good work." (1 Timothy 5:10)

While the above word speaks of what widows should do, it does show that helping the depressed and following all the good deeds is a Christian's work for all. Therefore, such brothers and sisters may not ask for help for many reasons. It is essential to help those in need by extending helping hands whenever we understand that this situation exists among some members and help them get out of such, even temporarily. And for this is the service of love, and a lover of his brother or sister should reveal in this way the true love he has. The primary purpose of our help should be to do what is pleasing to God by serving His will and mind.

"If a brother or sister be naked, and destitute of daily food, And one of you say unto them, depart in peace, be ye warmed and filled; notwithstanding ye give them not those things which are needful to the body; what doth it profits? Even so faith, if it hath not works, is dead, being alone." (James 2:15-17)

"Hereby perceive we the love of God, because he laid down his life for us: and we ought to lay down our lives for the brethren. But whoso hath this world's good, and seeth his brother has need, and shutteth up his bowels of compassion from him, how dwelleth the love of God in him? My little children, let us not love in word, neither in tongue; but indeed, and in truth." (1 John 3:16-18)

To serve by humbling oneself

It is an honour to be humbled to serve God. But unfortunately, many people don't seem to understand or want to know that. Because once they are assigned a place of service, some will be able to change their personality, treating even their close friends or others with contempt and displaying pride or arrogance. Arrogance is a sign of great weakness, lack of self-awareness, and not being mature with the mind. When the Lord Jesus taught the apostles about humility and humble service, He explained that He washed their feet at Easter.

The Lord Jesus told His apostles, after washing their feet, that if He washed their feet, while they call Him Lord and Teacher, they ought to wash each other's feet. We find this in John 13:14. The example tells them what the proverbs about obedience and demeaning say. The bottom line here in His ministry is to give to Him on behalf of the highest and almighty Creator of all things, that is, God. The service to the most significant and essential God must be humble, considering God's greatness. What is a mortal man? By what measure could he be compared to God? It is wrong to look down on anyone because every son of God is blessed. Since the servant is blessed and worthy of honour, he must show this in all his services.

"So after he had washed their feet, and had taken his garments, and was set down again, he said unto them, Know ye what I have done to you? Ye call me Master and Lord: and ye say well; for so I am. If I then, your Lord and Master, have washed your feet; ye also ought to wash one another's feet. For I have given you an example, that ye should do as I have done to you." (John 13:12-15)

Foot washing should be a way in which genuine humbleness of heart and respect are expressed to one another, not for formality or filming, but it must happen in a meaningful way in carrying out Christ's proper command.

Being a church elder, pastor, steward, shepherd, evangelist, teacher, apostle, prophet, deacon, singer, and other service givers in God's house should not be a position that gives superiority. On the contrary, considering other members as low esteemed people is not proper.

Of course, to accomplish and maintain the service they provide to members as they serve their assignments, all members of the house of God must respect their relationship with each other, and it must be appreciated by receiving, understanding, accepting, and obedience to each other.

It is well known and appropriate that members accept and obey their leaders' commands. Such acceptance should prevail among people of God with no difference between the people of God. Therefore, ministers need proper respect, help, and approval from members to serve in their appointed, assigned positions of responsibility adequately.

Leaders should not rule or act like authoritarian kings or rulers. Above all, they do not despise and wrongly treat their people. Healthy relationships can excel if they are respected, received, and trusted. Problems of breaking out of the church should not occur because of such a case which is the division and separation between members and the leadership. Separation is deliberate coercion from the enemy, and Christians must defend it. The problem can also stem from the flesh and the enemy. But since it can go in different ways, it is made plain in His Word that God does not love divisions.

"Now I beseech you, brethren, by the name of our Lord Jesus Christ, that ye all speak the same thing, and that there be no divisions among you; but that ye be perfectly joined together in the same mind and the same judgment." (1 Corinthians 1:10)

Therefore, these words urge in the Lord's name that there should not be a division among you. How would anyone who knows and reads these words then choose to break up the word? But, especially in this caution, the message to Galatians in the article above is that they must receive it.

So those who practice separation and seek separation are sinning. And if separation is a sin, sin's wages are death, so they have made their salvation in Christ a waste. Death means not the death of the flesh but death (the death of the spirit, which Adam died), and their salvation was in vain. Therefore, it is necessary to protect yourself from such failures.

Humbleness of mind calls for the most outstanding mani-festation of humility, obedience, love, and goodness in action in an impartial way to all people. That's not going to be as easy as what it says in the Bible. Man has under-served the kindness of the Lord and must decide to humble himself for the glory of the Lord. If he could not do it, he would fail in a way others have failed. The Lord's apostles acted as typical examples of this activity.

Their history, written in the book of Acts, tells us that they finished their time with the excellent work of the Lord humbly and lovingly. Otherwise, they would not have been able to carry out their great commission in their life. If they did not work in sheer sincerity with trust and love, inferiority, and self-obedience to the will of the Lord, their lives probably would not have perished. But they would not have accomplished even the smallest part of their assignment. Therefore, as Christ's followers today follow the Lord, we, too, must strive to fulfil our trust with the same responsibility and shouldering of burdens as the apostles.

This undignified personality must be for some service Christians may do in the church, but it is also a quality that each follower of Christ must have; one needs to travel with it like he keeps his finances.

Whosoever created having the image and appearance of God should receive and accommodate the other one, not by looking at the appearance or the situation, but without any differentiation and with equal consideration and attention in all that he can. When such happens, no matter how successful a life situation may be, we will have no difficulty keeping our heads down and serving others.

Wealth and success, or the diversity of knowledge and wisdom, should not be reasons for our variety. It is given to us by the Creator and is indulgent and available. Coming out of this world is necessary, but those in the Lord will finally meet in heaven. Since separation from this world can prevent us from entering God's Kingdom in heaven, it would be a better option to look forward to the future. Therefore, let all our ministry be in love and humbleness, for there is much more profit in heaven.

Let us check our living around non-believers

"That ye may walk honestly toward them that are without, and that ye may have lack of nothing." (1 Thessalonians 4:12)

"Having your conversation honest among the Gentiles: that, whereas they speak against you as evildoers, they may by your good works, which they shall behold, glorify God in the day of visitation." (1 Peter 2:12)

Disciples of Christ Jesus in this world are now living among us and society; we have a living style that we must show as we are going out and in, and this residing style we now live must preach the gospel and witness our life.

As we go out and meet non-gospel believers, we shall not condemn them for not living the correct gospel life. But, if they observe anything on us that can be disliked and criticised, they might develop the feelings and say things such as, 'If this is life in Christ, then I don't need it.' And then they may distance from us and the call of gospel and open the door for them not to accept the Lord. Our Christianity might become an obstacle to others.

This critical approach will be an awful reflection of being an obstacle to the will of the Lord and make us accountable on the day of judgement. We will be responsible for becoming an obstacle to those unbelievers who refuse because we are a stumbling block on things found in the way they see us and criticise us.

Our presence in His house is meaningless if we don't use the opportunity to make the Lord happy. Therefore, we shall be good examples for the Lord Jesus, who died for us, the one who gave us eternal life through His death and resurrection, so then we shall take care not to disappoint Him even to those under the control of the dark rule.

There are billions of people God created in His image and likeness from different languages and tribes worldwide. God knows everyone by name and resemblance.

God who created us has created them in the same way. God who created us gave us a great mind that can think, be knowledgeable, test and analyse, differentiate good from bad, the weak from the powerful, the honourable from the humiliated, and sin from righteousness. Knowledge is given to us in our hands to know and choose the best one from the worst. Because of this, many people choose the one that makes the flesh happy; others select the service with a suitable aroma, neglecting worldly joy and comfort but respecting living to the glory of the Lord. However, the gospel did come without these differences entrusting us in our hands. Hence, overcoming the designated task even if it requires sacrifice means we shall be prepared without preconditions and serve Him.

Most of the time, what we need is to focus on ourselves. It is essential to be prepared to pretext others' salvation spiritually. We must be engaged, well prepared, and equipped. To get this capacity the church must work. To qualify for such an effort, one must work with a coordinated effort from both sides but not happen as a role expected from the church alone. If members' willingness and preparedness are available, the church and the leaders must teach and train these members and deploy, and the result would be fruitful gospel work, no doubt.

The other issue we shall focus on is that we have many social reasons that connect us with others. What sort of role should we play when we meet in such relationships? For such questions as "How do we participate in situations where it needs our participation?", we can register some visible activity without receiving any criticism. We create a suitable condition to the name of the Lord and show the difference in our life, resulting in great chances. It should then be a chance we shall be happy to use.

When we meet with people from different religious groups, if we start telling them about their mistakes, they might get annoyed or disappointed and oppose us without first understanding what we say to them. So, fighting might mean putting a stumbling block on their way to salvation. Besides, Christians must not fight at all costs.

Our role should be to tell the salvation gospel and what Christ taught us. We should not oppose their religion at any cost. Instead, we need to pray in spirit when we witness people about Christ and ask the Holy Spirit to help the individual open his heart. Positively approaching them will help open the individual's heart to who we are seeing, allowing them to open their heart. If the individual is under the control of evil spirits, it will help them be free from sinful bondage. Our faith in the Lord has decisive results on what we are doing. If our faith is weak, the enemy can attack us; therefore, we shall try to be well prepared in prayer asking the Lord to help us in what we do and to grow in faith and know we will strengthen ourselves.

If the person we witness is short-tempered, we might go to the extent of taking forceful action; thus, we shall be well prepared not to get into such incidences. Instead, we shall carefully consider what we talk about and practice with wisdom and wise perception guided by the Holy Spirit. We should be careful and refrain from speaking about something that will make other people angry because the main objective is to bring people to salvation, not to make them angry. To do this, the Lord will help us with His grace, no doubt. If we must bring salvation to someone, we shall be doing this by patiently designing our communication as to how to start our conversation, where to start, and how to focus on such, which will help us achieve our objective. Instead of jumping right away to witness, it is better to start by developing a rapport built on common social background that allows us to create a good understanding, establish an agreement, and be open.

Therefore, creating such a situation is very important. It is thus possible to quote essential and vital verses from the gospel's New Testament after establishing a conducive condition for discussion after a conversation begins. If the person we witnessed is not immediately accepting, it is crucial to winning the debate by taking an alternate short appointment to continue the conversation.

We must pray for the next appointment and read salvation verses before approaching the person. We need to be ready without frustration until the unsaved person gets salvation with patience and vigilant explanations. Angels of heaven receive the newborn person by shouting and singing, apart from bringing out the individual from the darkness. We will also be profiting from this with the talent we are honoured.

"Likewise, I say unto you, there is joy in the presence of the angels of God over one sinner that repenteth." (Luke 15:10)

Therefore, let us be working for the gospel this way. Our relationship with unsaved people should be Holy, not drinking and eating or anything that is a useless worldly connection. Hence, the gospel should bring the unsaved people by witnessing the life we have, with the agreement, understanding, and showing them an exemplary life. If we can't do this, it means we haven't done fruitful work. With our lousy example, we must be cautious not to be an obstacle to the gospel; we should move carefully. In all these, we must walk without falling to sin; if we fall to such weakness, there is a protector that will lift us. Thus, for this unlimited help we get, the grace, from God, we shall thank Him.

CHAPTER 4

21. LET US CHECK OUR SOCIAL LIFE

In today's world, we cannot live without being connected to the outside social life; we cannot. Whether directly or indirectly, this social life psychologically impacts our lives in the short or long term.

Whether we like it or not, it is helpful to understand that we are not products of our family only but also society's expected results. Many studies indicate that man inherits most behaviours from the family (mainly from parents) and the community. When He created and made everything in the world, God did not create them the same way; the Bible tells us how He created man unlike all other things.

"And the Lord God formed man of the dust of the ground and breathed into his nostrils the breath of life, and man became a living soul." (Genesis 2:7)

Thus, it tells us we came from the soil in His own hands. But this is not the only thing that makes man special.

"So God created man in his image, in the image of God created he him; male and female created them." (Genesis 1:27)

As we have read above, He created man in His likeness and image. Therefore, God created us in His image and likeness. According to His Word, if we resemble Him, we shall live as cleanly as possible. A child born will grow, be educated, be employed, marry, and give birth to a child, which means the life cycle starts here. Suppose a person is born and grows to become mature (adult) in places other than the parent's home from the age of 18. In that case, the estimated age can also be from 20 to 30 years old (depending on the individual's society or tradition and custom); the results may differ between male and female individuals.

In these young adulthood ages, the experiences we acquire will help us go the rest of our lives, imposing some changes in our lives. Depending on the individual's condition, it can be that it takes user experiences for change to take place. It can be true in many people's lives and thoughts. More substantial, simple, or complex situations may occur in our lives. It is up to individuals to accept or reject the case, which depends on an individuals' power and strength, depending on the maturity and stability of the individual's mind. It is a grace given by God's unique gift. Because of this, we can't judge by asking why this one can do this or why the other one can't. Each one is walking according to who he is. Because God created each of us with a unique character, He made us different from others. Even our fingers are unique; our fingerprints are different and do not resemble another. Because God made it further, the world is using it to identify us, taking advantage of that.

God is extraordinary in His works; nobody can ask why He did it this way. His wisdom is sophisticated. Our difference is not supposed to create any separation, hate for each other, distance, or other. Not at all. For many of us, our parents' married life is our life experience, our expectation. Children will follow suit if the father and mother quarrel and fight. A similar situation can happen; if the father and mother live in perfect love, their children will follow that. But they can also be different from their parents.

Sometimes children might have the exact opposite character. It would be a mistake to always conclude that children will acquire the same feelings as their parents. Other factors will influence them, like the education they get from schools. Consider not quarrelling with people. Doing wrong to someone (which we do to one another), wrongly speaking, wrongly thinking, mischief, envy, jealousy, conspiracy, insult, drunkenness, addiction to different substances, laziness, and killing someone are hated experiences we know and should avoid. We should try to run away from characters such as these and others. We should know that if we fall into committing one of these, we can die eternal death because of our sins. Our only refuge is Jesus Christ, and we should run into His armpit (repentance) to shelter; that is our only choice.

With our spouse (man to the woman, woman to the man only), the healthy life they share has contributed significantly to life. So, for marriage to be successful, it must be healthy and have a positive attitude to each other.

Of course, the Bible says in Ephesians 5:22-31 that after being a Christian, if you do not obey the Word of God, then what you are worshipping is something else, not the true God. Christians can only prove their Christianity by living according to the gospel. After knowing the Word, if he cannot live according to it or tries to interpret it according to his feeling, he is putting himself far from the true path and fooling himself. Christianity is something you live and expose yourself to according to the Word but not something nominal where you don't respect the Word and the faith; it shall not be at all. We must be careful not to be swiped away by any wind that blows and goes out of our track; we shall be cautious from such. The Word warns us this way.

"That we henceforth are no more children tossed to and fro, and carried about with every wind of doctrine, by the sleight of men, and cunning craftiness, whereby they lie in wait to deceive." (Ephesians 4:14)

Divorce occurs due to conflict between the husband and the wife resulting from a misunderstanding. The devil's effort is to dismantle marriage permanently, at any cost. Because family is the foundation of churches, Satan always tries to develop the problem. Quarrels can happen for a simple reason: the individuals didn't try to avoid or discuss with each other and resolve on time. Then because of this situation (either the two or one of them) may not have tried to avoid it.

If we give it time, even the slightest issue, the devil can widen the gap between ideas and start working diligently to stand against each other. Husband and wife come from families with different backgrounds. It is wrong to think of them as having the same behaviour. Many times, we find them to be different in many ways.

Every human being is known to have one of these behaviours in life. Whether they are married or in any other relationship who know each other, if they disagree, their unity will be under stress because they cannot accommodate each other's feelings or ideas. Their difference will increase because they cannot be patient; they do not want to be controlled by others. They may not want to be governed by the Word of God, accept each other, and become winners by understanding each other. If a couple prays together when they have something they have disagreed on within their heart, a difference in idea, or anything that disappointed the other, they must come to ask forgiveness before the Lord.

If they do this, the enemy cannot defeat them and keep regrets accumulating. If husband and wife cannot control themselves this way, one can be a victim of the enemy, open doors, and enter freely to attack them. The devil will work hard until he dismantles the marriage and will not stop until he succeeds. Christians need to know this. Christians should know this very well and understand the devil's work to destroy them and their union, and they should be doing everything possible against the devil to live a peaceful life.

Suppose a husband is trying to be dominant over the wife based on societal norms and shows superiority outside the Word of God, not administering his house as per God's Word by imposition (male dominancy). In that case, that will be a mistake. A woman doesn't recognise the husband as the head in life, and if the man doesn't respect the wife, this will create disagreement. Such a situation will aggravate and open doors to the enemy, creating conflict that will create an unfavourable situation for both; this may lead to divorce, enhancing the separation between the couple.

Therefore, we must carefully handle our marriage life as we live through society. Before accusing and condemning each other for the fault made, the husband or wife should stop and check the cause of the problem, and work on the situation carefully by asking the question, "What if I am the cause?" and try to check oneself and try to solve the problem, which will be better. Then, they can settle the situation and solve the problem together, saving them from an issue that would have destroyed their marriage.

There are incidences where only Satan can be the cause, but it would be wrong to think that way always. There are instances where problems can be created mistakenly by us, which emanates from us not understanding how it can when we take our steps by affecting our spouse and harming other friends. It won't quickly solve the problem unless it tries to check itself. Most of the time, people fail to accept when someone tells them about their mistake because they think they are right. As the Lord spoke out in His words, we shall go and ask forgiveness before we kneel for prayer if we have some trespasses. No one is supposed to interpret this word in any other way to give a different meaning. If we can't forgive, God will not forgive us. It will not be a mistake to say many people fail to forgive, although they know well and continue carrying their lives shouldering their trespass.

"Leave there thy gift before the altar, and go thy way; first be reconciled to thy brother, and then come and offer thy gift." (Matthew 5:24)

Thus, if they do not follow the Word and practice it, which faith are they following? As the Lord said, we should obey His Word, but by giving our reasons, if we do not forgive those who trespassed us, which Christianity are we following? Christianity is the life we live for our sake. It is not a life we live to make other people happy. The Lord has told us to receive the eternal life He prepared for us by following and keeping His commandments for our sake. As said through His sacred word, it is foolish to keep on trespassing, not forgiving others who trespassed; it is useless if you think God knows your heart. It is foolishness that is worse than we ever believe. Otherwise, God has made it clear that He doesn't work and goes with those that do not obey His words in many ways. Therefore, God has spoken that He will not cooperate with those that do not obey His commandments. Consequently, we cannot make God happy without following His Word; knowing otherwise that He will not answer our request is wise. The words we use to make it look the right way may bring us judgement; otherwise, it may not save us from God's judgement.

"For whosoever shall be ashamed of me and of my words, of him shall the Son of man be ashamed, when he shall come in his own glory, and in his Father's, and of the holy angels." (Luke 9:26)

"If ye love me, keep my commandments. And I will pray for the Father, and he shall give you another Comforter, that he may abide with you forever." (John 14:15-16)

When we receive the Lord, if we ignore the precious thing given to us and our focus remains on worldly issues, we should know that the result is inevitable loss. God is not like a human; no one can cheat Him because He cares for His glory and His name.

"Ye shall not go after other gods, of the gods of the people which are round about you; (For the Lord thy God is a jealous God among you) lest the anger of the Lord thy God be kindled against thee, and destroy thee from off the face of the earth." (Deuteronomy 6:14-15)

Therefore, if any man wants to follow and worship Him, it should be with great carefulness. But, on the other hand, if we live the way we want, as if we are clean people while practicing all sorts of worldly things, then we are inviting danger to ourselves because we cannot mock God, as expressed in the following verse:

"Be not deceived; God is not mocked: for whatsoever a man soweth, that shall he also reap." (Galatians 6:7)

God will make us harvest what we broadcast. If you plant *teff*[1] you can't reap *dagusa*, or if you plant maize and harvest sorghum, or plant beans and harvest peas. God can only make you grow, germinate, flower, and bear fruits, and if anything happens outside this, it could be a dream or nightmare but not something of reality.

We should be worshipping our God and respecting the commandments He gave us. We must live around that because our life and worship cannot go separately. Finding them separated shows that we have a problem, but it can't be a better way.

Whether personal or societal, our relationships should glorify the Lord but not tarnish His name, and we shall be careful not to have such harmful consequences. We will end up blaming the name of the Lord if, in the house of the Lord, we don't check our way of living and act without considering whether it glorifies our Lord or not. So, for this not to happen we should be careful when we go about our everyday activities, with our living, communication with people, what we do even when we talk we should think, evaluate, and take care very well.

We should walk so they can see the Lord revealed in us as people could see in our lives. But, indeed, it is not easy to do this as written here. It, of course, requires carrying the Cross daily and following His path.

---

[1] *Teff* = a grass-like crop which is staple food in Ethiopia. The seeds are tiny, just smaller than mustard fruit. The scientific name is *eragrostce tef.*

Carrying the Cross will involve paying sacrifice and demands strong discipline. However, it is not something impossible. Because His grace is there to help us on our way, for those who are determined, even if it needs sacrifice, many strong people have managed to walk in this way successfully, and there could be others who will do so too.

Therefore, we need to pass through the narrow gate daily, walking under His Cross, and when we do so, He will help us with His grace that will enable us to reach the height He destined for us.

Since family is the foundation of the church, the devil focuses more on attacking marriages. Therefore, we need to consciously try to prevent the attack on a church by protecting the family from being attacked by the devil. It is a secret to the public that many marriages are suffering from the enemy attack because that comes from the enemy in the form of disagreements between spouses, making them live a miserable life on earth. Christian husband condemns the wife, and the wife blames the husband without knowing the cause of their disagreement. The enemy is the cause of the problem and lives on earth under attack, suffering, living apart from each other and engaging in conflict, causing their marriage to falter. Therefore, we must stop thinking about God's words and protect our marriage from the enemy's attack.

"For the Lord, the God of Israel, saith that he hateth putting away: for one covereth violence with his garment, saith the Lord of hosts: therefore take heed to your spirit, that ye deal not treacherously." (Malachi 2:16)

"Art thou bound unto a wife? seek not to be loosed. Art thou loosed from a wife? Seek not a wife." (1 Corinthians 7:27)

Honestly, it may not be appropriate to consider Satan the reason for our disagreement because we also have opportunities to play the role ourselves. Everyone has unusual behaviour. However, one who is born again through Jesus Christ is more capable of spiritually controlling fleshly temptations through self-governing and checking themselves better than others. Because it is the way the flesh is behaving, one must avoid and create a favourable situation for the spouse (male or female) and develop a healthy marriage. The powerful thing here could be that each person needs to know and understand his behaviour and listen to what others say about him. Finding a solution to the problem starts with understanding and accepting the problem's accurate picture. No one who counts himself as correct and absolute will have this opportunity. No one on earth is correct and complete except Jesus Christ; no one will ever be.

"But we are all as an unclean thing, and all our righteousnesses are as filthy rags, and we all do fade as a leaf; and our iniquities, like the wind, have taken us away." (Isaiah 64:6)

We can control ourselves; our capability is through Christ Jesus who paid the price for our sins and redeemed us from sin. He is the one who protects us from evil. Therefore, we shall not spoil the chance to accomplish the useless fleshly need. It will be abusing or underestimating God. But our God is God who is jealous of His glory; He will not ignore those who attack Him even though He is merciful in punishing those who trespass. So here is where we must be cautious.

Suppose the judgement is not made by God immediately for the sin that we have committed because God was quiet about it, delaying His decision. In that case, it doesn't mean He is allowing us time to continue, but we should be returning and repenting. It does not mean we get pardoned without judging us for our trespasses and sin. It shall not lead us to ignore or undermine Him, for He delayed acting; instead, it shows His patience, that He is accommodating, and with fear and trembling shall we return and live in the right way of life. For this God that we are governed by, we shall show that we are obedient, sanctified for Him, that we are obedient to Him, and if we don't show these and practice in our living and hold it as our treasure, remember it will not make God happy at all; we must show that in life.

"For as the body without the spirit is dead, so faith without works is dead also." (James 2:26)

Therefore, there is no better chance than diligently practicing what one knows and has learnt in life, the faith that one has received. If this doesn't happen, one who cannot prove his faith practically will expose himself to danger. Whichever reason given for not fulfilling or keeping the commandment will not be accepted. The decision will be the individual's. According to his faith or the destruction, the result he gets depends on the individual's responsibility. God will never be responsible; because He has given everyone the capacity to think and decide for himself. He has given each one a giant brain that can think, research, and understand. Since God is God of freedom, God wants us to worship Him freely. He has never forced anyone or attracted anyone to honour Him. If He was doing this, people worldwide should have worshipped only one God. Therefore, let us use this opportunity to escape from judgement and destruction.

CHAPTER 5

22. LET US CHECK OUR RELATIONSHIP AND LIFE WITH THE LORD

How is our relationship with the Lord? The Lord taught and led us through the word to resemble Him, not to follow our own way or to create a favourable situation for our fleshly living. Of course, should we need to live an undefeated life in this world with a victory?

Is this something possible? To those who question this, yes, it is possible. Because some people played an exemplary role by living as per His words and died, there are more people today that may commit themselves for such. However, if we are looking for comfort and peace in this world, we cannot fulfil what we are supposed to live according to the gospel and live a righteous life that will help us inherit Heaven. If this happens, our life will be missing its target. It means we will be missing the prepared crown of glory for us. Let the Lord protect us from such.

The Lord Jesus Christ will always be with those of us who believe in Him. He has promised us, saying, "I will be with you until the end of the world" (as it says in Matthew 28:19-20). The Lord is faithful to His word.

"Go ye therefore, and teach all nations, baptizing them in the name of the Father, and of the Son, and of the Holy Ghost: Teaching them to observe all things whatsoever I have commanded you: and, lo, I am with you always, even unto the end of the world." (Matthew 28:19-20)

His existence, presence, visitation, help, rescue, protection, mercy, blessings all of these assure us that He is with us.

One who has prepared himself for greater visitation correctly will receive anointing from the Holy Spirit, this is what he deserves to get. This spirituality, of course, will pave the way for our communication. Thus, we should follow it with concern. Christianity separated from Christ will be meaningless, and we may not have anything called Christianity. In life, we must provide additional space to check if our life resembles Christ Jesus and confirm if it is clear and that it is easy. But when the Lord said He is helpful, He is trustful to help us by generously providing His support. Our faith in Him is sufficient to move to resemble Him. What follows next to faith is practicing our faith. When this happens, a complete Christ-life may be visible in our lives, and we have identified ourselves to resemble the Lord.

If our life doesn't resemble Christ, we can't say we are Christians. If we lead our lives in this worldly way, we cannot say we have a life that resembles Christ's, as one cannot be for two different masters. We also cannot be servants to this world (Satan's) and the Lord's; we can't be servants to both simultaneously because one who is a servant to Satan cannot be the servant of God. One servant of God cannot be a servant to Satan. When the Lord was teaching, he said nobody can be a servant of two masters.

"No man can serve two masters: for either he will hate the one and love the other; or else he will hold to the one, and despise the other. Ye cannot serve God and mammon." (Matthew 6:24)

In our life on earth, when we look at those things created for human beings and the level of civilisation that we have reached, it doesn't mean that we should not use the development that we have built in the past, but we need to see in what way and how we can use it carefully. For example, if our children watch films on TV, some might be obsessed with the evil spirit and may adopt something wrong from the enemy. Maybe if you are mature in His words, your thinking might help you notice the sin you are committing from the righteous life you are living. Differentiating the humiliation from the honourable and examining it may help you oppose and break the bondage; you may use it wisely. But if we watch films in a situation where such a condition doesn't exist, we might also be attracted to it and serve the devil's plan. We can imagine how it impacts our children if this can happen to mentally grown people. Because such can happen to our children, it becomes evident that more destruction is happening to them in many other ways. We need to resemble the Lord through solid discipline in our relationship with the Lord and our lives. Considering what has been told to us in His Word, betraying Satan and the world, killing the flesh with its lust, and moving towards receiving our eternal life by believing the Lord, we shall move forward to live with Him till the end. It is not as easy as it says here in the idea, but it is supposed to work through how we live. Faith separated from action is dead.

"For as the body without the spirit is dead, so faith without works is dead also." (James 2:260)

If we can't practice what we have learnt here, who are we expecting to do it? Some misunderstand this and say His grace saves us, and we must do nothing, but this is a great mistake. The word hereunder tells us that faith must work as sufficient evidence. We know what grace can do to us. It is to help us stand undefeated when fleshly lust tests us, to get the power to shy away from sin, to be able to stand against resisting tests, but not that we move as we like to fulfil the fleshly lust and not disprove our faith by simply following our desires.

"Even so faith, if it hath not works, is dead, being alone." (James 2:17)

It is the right and perfect path to express ourselves to show that we are in a relationship with the Lord in a most confirming way. On the contrary, not expressing our faith indicates that we are leading our life suspiciously and questionably. Our life, living as we desire, is not conforming to the life we are in with the Lord. Many non-Christians live a comfortable life relaxed in this world.

Troubles, problems, and tests can happen, but we may not wish to have a dominating life. However, we should know that such situations are more imposing on Christians than the non-believers. Therefore, it is better to know and be ready for such a test that will be on those who believe the Word and live accordingly on earth.

"These things I have spoken unto you, that in me ye might have peace. In the world ye shall have tribulation: but be of good cheer; I have overcome the world." (John 16:33)

Our Christian life journey is to resemble that of His son, Jesus Christ. We don't have any option other than resembling Christ. We will remain short of His glory if we do not choose this and prepare ourselves for this. No one can cheat God like He can cheat human beings. He is righteous in His judgement. He is all knowledgeable.

Therefore, why do we have to simulate ourselves for our advantage? Not even pastors or preachers if we say should not be. Why do we have to live the way we want in the church? The way we worship, the way we keep our righteousness, the way we avoid sin, the way we pay our tithe, the way we conduct different fellowship programs, and the way we serve Him, we must obey and make Him happy. Any idea that will make us discard this develops into a negative attitude. The source will not be from the Lord; thus, we must check ourselves and be able to return to the Lord immediately.

Those who find it difficult to differentiate the fleshly thought from the spiritual and yet think what they have in mind or whatever they feel is right to serve the Lord as correct to avoid coming to church should know that it is not the right way.

The one that works to separate the people from God is the devil but not God. God will not separate His people at all. The Word never supports separation but tells us to accommodate each other, love and hold each other, and continue. God never works to expel anyone from His house. Before removing anyone from the church, the church leaders' first step should be to advise the person and warn them. But if the person doesn't want to be corrected, then better avoid him before he affects others; the church must do this to keep the congregants' healthy relations safe. Everybody must pray for such a person until the end so that the Lord returns him.

If the person commits a mistake that will expel him from church, what can we pray to God to solve the problem and make him stand with faith? After taking a stand we should continue our fellowship. It does not mean it will happen in our flesh in the time frame we think. We shall wait for the time of God with patience. It is the right road that will keep our relationship with the Lord. But if we follow the way we think is suitable for us without asking God, our decision will be outside the Word, which will undoubtedly damage us. We must be cautious to help us avoid clashing with our God and trespassing with our choices and actions. We must walk with the Lord by knowing His will, keeping His Word, obeying self-governance with the right heart and humility.

23. WHEN AND HOW DO WE NEED BEHAVIOURAL CHANGE, AND IN WHAT CONDITION?

There is a behaviour that God put in us when He created us. However, from the time we are born, from our childhood age until we grow old, there could be a change in our behaviour. The behaviour born with us in childhood may stay unchanged until we die. The behaviour we acquire from life from the time we are born is more significant after the Holy Spirit controls us through Jesus. There is a considerable difference between the two. The one that can enter Heaven is the one that is born from water and Spirit.

"Jesus answered, Verily, verily, I say unto thee, except a man be born of water and the Spirit, he cannot enter into the kingdom of God." (John 3:5)

One who has accepted Jesus Christ as his Saviour must express his faith by taking baptism and being filled with the Holy Spirit. When someone gets Jesus as his Saviour, immediately the Holy Spirit starts revealing itself in him. It is not an assumption, but it is the truth we can now see happening. In many ways, the Holy Spirit reveals itself in many believers. Speaking in tongues is the main sign seen in many new believers. Different spiritual anointings will start to happen to many believers. When this grace comes in a definite way, the person can serve as a teacher, evangelist, prophet, apostle, elder, deacon, singer, and pastor, and they will start doing the Lord. These are ways of new behavioural changes. The newborn person in Jesus Christ becomes a new creation through the baptism of water and

Spirit and cannot be the same fleshly person because the person has been changed and becomes a new creation.

"Therefore if any man be in Christ, he is a new creature: old things are passed away; behold, all things have become new." (2 Corinthians 51:7)

Suppose a person continues living in the same old fleshly life and persists in the same behaviour; in that case, this person may have been following someone or wanted to join for some benefit. God can examine the heart and kidney; thus, we can't escape. Therefore, no one can tell Him lies. So, it is because God can read everything, see, and be everywhere simultaneously.

"I know that thou canst do everything, and that no thought can be withholden from thee." (Job 42:2)

Our old being cannot continue as it is; thus, as it says above, after we become a new creation by accepting Jesus, our old being is changed into an unknown. We must drop the old behaviour and try to hold on to the new life. Therefore, we must get relieved quickly from our worldly life and start our new journey. There are many obstacles the new believer will face in this new journey. To overcome these obstacles, the one who fights him will mainly be the devil, but the believer may also have a problem as he tries to escape the old being and fails. The decisive step would be fasting and prayer by asking the help of the Lord to stand firm without losing hope and continue in faith with the Lord.

23.1   The true Christian image

What is the actual image of a Christian one should have? Individuals can give answers with different views from their perspectives. The individual can provide the solution based on the other pictures and measurements to define the proper response from a biblical perspective. We cannot argue on biblical words that arise any argument. Interpretation of the Word may raise questions. Here, the Word is used in simple language to avoid unnecessary disputes. The main thing here is understanding the truth, not politics, having the upper hand, or winning ideas to suppress others' opinions. Above all, the Holy Bible will witness the reality for the reader. Therefore, there is no need to present any strengthening idea. Though following actual Christian wording can be in muscular terms, it applies to both men and women.

- Christian is a disciple of Christ.

  "Go ye therefore, and teach all nations, baptizing them in the name of the Father, and of the Son, and of the Holy Ghost: Teaching them to observe all things whatsoever I have commanded you: and, lo, I am with you always, even unto the end of the world." (Matthew 28:19-20)

- Is far from enjoying worldly sin and lust.

  "But God be thanked, that ye were the servants of sin, but ye have obeyed from the heart that form of doctrine which was delivered you. Being then made free from sin, ye became the servants of righteousness." (Romans 6:17-18)

"Wherefore if ye be dead with Christ from the rudiments of the world, why, as though living in the world, are ye subject to ordinances, Touch not; taste not; handle not." (Colossians 2:20-21)

- Endures tribulation, patiently accommodates it.

"Blessed is the man that endureth temptation: for when he is tried, he shall receive the crown of life, which the Lord hath promised to them that love him." (James 1:12)

- Has the heart of the Lord, loves people with true love.

"For who hath known the mind of the Lord, that he may instruct him? But we have the mind of Christ." (1 Corinthians 2:16)

- Diligent in prayer always.

"Praying always with all prayer and supplication in the Spirit, and watching thereunto with all perseverance and supplication for all saints." (Ephesians 6:18)

- Honest, hard-working, and diligent.

"Exhort servants to be obedient unto their masters, and to please them well in all things; not answering again; Not purloining, but shewing all good fidelity;

that they may adorn the doctrine of God our Savior in all things." (Titus 2:9-10)

- Upright in his heart, he always wants to help people.

  "Masters, give unto your servants that which is just and equal; knowing that ye also have a Master in heaven." (Colossians 4:1)

  "Or he that exhorteth, on exhortation: he that giveth, let him do it with simplicity; he that ruleth, with diligence; he that sheweth mercy, with cheerfulness." (Romans 12:8)

- Honest in the house of God, pays tithe loyalty.

  "Will a man rob God? Yet ye have robbed me. But ye say, wherein have we robbed thee? In tithes and offerings." (Malachi 3:8)

- Accepts any assignment given from church and serves for the sake of the Lord.

  "I beseech you therefore, brethren, by the mercies of God, that ye present your bodies a living sacrifice, holy, acceptable unto God, which is your reasonable service." Romans 12:1

- Serves the house of God with complete will with the anointing God gave him.

  "Or ministry, let us wait on our ministering: or he that teacheth, on teaching." (Romans 12:7)

- Studies the word of God regularly; tries to live according to the word he understood always.

  "And Jesus answered him, saying, It is written, That man shall not live by bread alone, but by every word of God." (Luke 4:4)

  "So then faith cometh by hearing and hearing by the word of God." (Romans 10:17)

- He puts all hopes in God and lives in faith, believing his God.

  "And David was greatly distressed; for the people spake of stoning him, because the soul of all the people was grieved, every man for his sons and his daughters: but David encouraged himself in the Lord his God." (1 Samuel 30:6)

- He doesn't count on a trespass, forgives who trespassed, and asks forgiveness from those he trespassed.

  "Doth not behave itself unseemly, seeketh not her own, is not easily provoked, thinketh no evil." (1 Corinthians 13:5)

  "But if ye do not forgive, neither will your Father which is in heaven forgive your trespasses." (Mark 11:26)

- Makes an effort to help with everything possible for those who live in abject poverty life.

  "Well reported of for good works; if she have brought up children, if she have lodged strangers, if she have washed the saints' feet, if she have relieved the afflicted, if she have diligently followed every good work." (1 Timothy 5:10)

- As written in the world, believes he is a new creation and tries to live in this.

  "Therefore if any man be in Christ, he is a new creature: old things are passed away; behold, all things are become new." (2 Corinthians 5:17)

- Lives a victorious life believing in Jesus and winning devil pride.

  "Being born again, not of corruptible seed, but of incorruptible, by the word of God, which liveth and abideth forever." (1 Peter 1:23)

- Never gets defeated to world joy and pleasure but lives looking forward to eternal happiness.

  "For the kingdom of God is not meat and drink, but righteousness, peace, and joy in the Holy Ghost." (Romans 14:17)

- Never speaks unmannered, but will weigh, think and carefully speak.

  "Let no corrupt communication proceed out of your mouth, but that which is good to the use of edifying, that it may minister grace unto the hearers." (Ephesians 4:29)

  "If any man among you seem to be religious, and bridleth, not his tongue, but deceiveth his own heart, this man's religion is vain." (James 1:26)

- In marriage, lives with honesty limited to one (man/woman) according to the Word of God.

  "For this cause shall a man leave his father and mother and shall be joined unto his wife, and they two shall be one flesh." (Ephesians 5:31)

- Is an excellent example of living in life socially and as an individual that resembles Christ Jesus, like a perfect example of God.

  "Teaching us that, denying ungodliness and worldly lusts, we should live soberly, righteously, and godly, in this present world; Looking for that blessed hope, and the glorious appearing of the great God and our Savior Jesus Christ." (Titus 2:12-13)

- In times of trouble and tests, he relies on God.

  "Let Israel hope in the Lord: for with the Lord there is mercy, and with him is plenteous redemption." (Psalm 130:7)

  "Trust in the Lord, and do good; so shalt thou dwell in the land, and verily thou shalt be fed." (Psalm 37:3)

- Forgives all people who trespassed by leaving for God, who will judge.

  "For we know him that hath said, Vengeance belongeth unto me, I will repay, saith the Lord. And again, The Lord shall judge his people." (Hebrews 10:30)

- He uses the anointing received from the Lord not to glorify himself but for the fame and reputation of Christ.

  "Heal the sick, cleanse the lepers, raise the dead, cast out devils: freely ye have received, freely give." (Matthew 10:8)

- He gives priority to the will of God in his life, work, generally, in his walk of life.

  "Paul, a servant of Jesus Christ, called to be an apostle, separated unto the gospel of God (which he had promised afore by his prophets in the holy scriptures)" (Romans 1:1)

- Endureth tests, walks in faith in the Lord, understands the direction of the enemy, and never gives himself up to the attack of evil.

  "Blessed is the man that endureth temptation: for when he is tried, he shall receive the crown of life, which the Lord hath promised to them that love him." (James 1:12)

- Diligent in trying to witness the gospel of Jesus Christ to unsaved people, ready to pay the sacrifice for this.

  "And ye shall be hated of all men for my name's sake: but he that endureth to the end shall be saved." (Matthew 10:22)

  "For whosoever will save his life shall lose it; but whosoever shall lose his life for my sake and the gospel's, the same shall save it." (Mark 8:35)

- Generally, he leads his life in righteousness and holiness, focuses on that, and has no condemnation for any sin.

  "Do all things without murmurings and disputings: That ye may be blameless and harmless, the sons of God, without rebuke, during a crooked and perverse nation, among whom ye shine as lights in the world." (Philippians 2:14-15)

Indeed, the points mentioned above do not mean it explains all characteristics of true Christians; however, some of the main points presented here may be useful. Taking these points as the basis, you can add other holy points.

Here the question is to respond reasonably to such demanding issues; how much attention do we give to practice them in our life and walkthrough? That is the question.

23.2   The false (impersonator) Christian image

"in perils among false brethren." (2 Corinthians 1:26)

Judas was an impersonator. Judas tried to impersonate the disciples of Jesus Christ. Eventually, he became a betrayer, cheater, and murderer. Satan entered Judas among the twelve disciples, and he consulted the officials of the synagogue and heads of priests about how he could hand over the Lord to them. They were happy; then they agreed to pay him. He agreed; he was looking for a convenient time when people would come together to hand him over. After prayer, He got up and came to the disciples when He found them asleep due to heavy sadness, and He asked them why they sleep. Then He commented, "Get up and pray lest you enter temptation." While just as He was speaking, people came, and one of the disciples, Judas, was ahead of them; and approached to kiss Him. But Jesus said to him, "Do you hand over the son of man?" (Luke 22:3-6; 6:45-48)

Absalom was an impersonator. When Absalom invited his brother, he imitated as if he loved him, but the end of the invitation had a conspiracy. The invitation he made was a plot to kill his brother and make it a destructive act. Since he was ashamed of his sister Tamar, Absalom hated him, but he never said good or bad about him. After two years, Absalom invited all his father's children after the sheep sheered his sheep's furs near Baal-Hazor, beside Ephraim. Absalom came to his father and asked him if he would go sheer sheep to come with Absalom and all other servants. But the king said to Absalom, "My son, we all will burden you; thus, we can't go to you." Absalom insisted on his demand; he blessed him but refused to go. Then Absalom saw that he was going and begged to send his brother Amnon. Then the king asked him why he should go with him. But Absalom insisted; thus, the king trusted him and sent Amnon with his servants and children. Absalom gave a feast like that of a king, and he told his servants to watch when Amnon is drunk and is very happy and kill him. "When I say kill him, do not be afraid, am I not who ordered you? Be courageous and firm." So, the servants of Absalom did as he asked of them on Amnon. All the children of the king got on their mule and fled (see: 2 Samuel 13:22-29).

It is hard to say someone is a false Christian (impersonator) because if someone knows that he has accepted Christ as a saviour, the next thing that happens is they change from their old type of life. After testing a life in Christ and understanding the price paid for Him, no one would want to continue in the old kind of life. However, some people have got problems which will not help them live according to the Word. Among the issues, the following are some:

- Those who have witnessed and received Christ but cannot come out of the old way of life because they are with addictions and can still be in their old ways.

- Sometimes, when the correct foundation of Christian faith teaching may not be given and only followed with some preaching, they may remain living in the old being.
- Not knowing exactly why they accepted Christ, and without understanding, may result in following people whom they take as an example because they want to be like them and so they join the Christian church.
- Their family may be members of the church, therefore, take it as some inheritance considering the faith belongs to the family and they follow without a personal decision.
- Some may follow because many people admire Christianity and follow it by imitating others without understanding.
- They became members because they saw miracles and healing or wanted to receive healing for their sickness and, when cured, remained in the church.
- Those who do not read the Word; even if they read, do not understand very well and never experienced how to live according to the Word.
- Individuals devote themselves to fasting and prayer but do not know how to obey the Holy Spirit.
- Those who did not learn the Christian ways of teaching that are given in the church with particular emphasis and do not follow regularly.

These types of people are among those who do not reflect the Christian image. When such happens, those non-believer people, by seeing and noticing how they behave, would say, "If this is their faith, then why should we follow their faith?", and they try to shy away. The result can be an obstacle to others who want to come to the Lord. It is why 'not true (impersonator) Christians' was mentioned above to indicate the difference.

"They profess that they know God; but in works they deny him, being abominable, and disobedient, and unto every good work reprobate." (Titus 1:16)

In what ways do the non-true (impersonate) Christians differ from others? We will look at history for points on this as follows (since the reference verses are the same as given for the true Christians except for a few similar corresponding verses and will be taken as is.)

- They never count themselves as disciples; they are not ready for such.

  "And he that taketh not his cross, and followeth after me, is not worthy of me." (Matthew 10:38)

- He has not been able to depart from his old being, he regularly does sin in secret.

  "He that covereth his sins shall not prosper: but whoso confesseth and forsaketh them shall have mercy." (Proverbs 28:13)

- He doesn't have the heart that can love other people in him because he doesn't have the heart of the Lord.

  "Though I speak with the tongues of men and angels, and have not charity, I have become as sounding brass or a tinkling cymbal." (1 Corinthians 13:1)

- He doesn't pray regularly and doesn't make an effort to pray.
- He is not trustworthy and is affected by laziness.

"The foolishness of man perverteth his way: and his heart fretteth against the Lord." (Proverbs 19:3)

"The thought of foolishness is sin: the scorner is an abomination to men." (Proverbs 24:9)

- He is not upright with his heart; this evil, like he was in his old being, doesn't help men and doesn't have charity.

"Let us draw near with a true heart in full assurance of faith, having our hearts sprinkled from an evil conscience, and our bodies washed with pure water." (Hebrews 10:22)

- He does not have the will to serve in the house of the Lord and does not pay his tithe.

"Ye have said, It is vain to serve God: What profit is it that we have kept his ordinance and walked mournfully before the Lord of hosts?" (Malachi 3:14)

- He runs away from church services and doesn't want to serve the Lord.
- He doesn't know which one is an anointment of God, even if he knows he doesn't want to serve.
- He doesn't show diligence to study the Word of the Lord, doesn't live in what he understood, and never shows willingness.

- His hope on God is until he finds favourable situations; his faith depends upon what he gains.
- Counts on transgressions have a problem forgiving those who ask forgiveness; he feels challenged to ask forgiveness from those he harmed.
- He doesn't have the keen heart to help troubled people.
- He doesn't believe he is a new creation through Christ Jesus and lives accordingly.
- He doesn't know he is born from an unperishable seed and is open to the devil's test.
- He exposes himself to worldly joy and comfort and finds it challenging to comply with the heavenly.
- He never cares for his speech, is tested with laziness, and quarrels with people. As a result, he quickly falls under adultery sin very easily, does not lead his marriage rightly, and never shows according to the Word of God.
- Since he doesn't have a life that resembles Christ, he doesn't learn lessons from Jesus' unbelievers.
- Instead of asking God during troubled and tested times, he presents his problems to the fleshly man.
- He is ready to take revenge but not to forgive people who trespassed him; he wants to take vengeance himself.
- If there is any anointing given from God, he will try to use it for his advantage.
- He uses his social life's relationships to try have the feeling of serving his own needs.
- He quickly falls under temptation from his faith, cannot walk straight believing the Lord, doesn't understand the devil's aim, and promptly exposes himself to the enemy attack.

- He doesn't dare to witness Christ Jesus to unsaved ones and is unwilling to pay the sacrifice he must pay for this.
- Generally, he doesn't try to lead his life in righteousness and holiness, which looks failed in almost every field of his life.

Therefore, as presented briefly, the above points hint at Christianity's correct and incorrect type, but it has many more explanations. Generally, what you read above compares the true and the false Christian.

Hence, as explained above, those who follow Christianity incorrectly could be without understanding why they wanted to be Christian followers and not knowing what sacrifice it requires, why they follow, and what it entails.

It is disappointing because no one can satisfy God and, above all, cannot receive the blessings and healing obtained from God. So many have been affected walking in this way.

The enemy might have attacked their lives and affected them, creating confusion and trouble. So, they are short of eternal life. For someone who may think these people are Christians, they come to church and try to participate in different church activities. But whatever they do, they are doing it to synchronise with others, but not to obey faithfully and spiritually and not emanating from a keen sense of serving the Lord.

When a substantial assignment comes, they hide, giving lame excuses, not being able, and generally, they can be hiding. But, above all, they have mostly been criticised for a defiled exemplary life.

These people count themselves as correct and engaged in criticising far better than them and condemn them in many other ways. They blame them, usually based on false accusations tarnishing the name of others. They serve the enemy; however, they shelter under the shadow of the mercy of the Lord. This type does not qualify for the house of God and defiles the glory and status of the Lord, making His Spirit an obstacle not to work. Because the Holy Spirit does not operate in a place where it is an unholy situation, it means the problem goes beyond the individual to affect the whole congregation as well as the house of God.

Therefore, to return such Christians and believers, it is possible to correct them by advising and counselling them. If they are going to be left to move freely, it can reach a stage where the disadvantage is greater than the benefit. If they are going to be led astray, the weakness can disturb the spiritual life of other members.

Those who do not follow a Christian life and those who affect the lives of others, as far as the church knows them, clearly must be taught a lesson to live a life beneficial to the Lord, themselves, and their holiness. Efforts to prevent those who become obstacles to others will prevent them from doing so. Measures must change people's lives, correct them, give them advice, warn them, and discipline them to fix them continuously. If the person cannot update through all these efforts, we shall consider this as some heathen, and you can go up to purging/neglect from church.

"And if he shall neglect to hear them, tell it unto the church: but if he neglect to hear the church, let him be unto thee as a heathen man and a publican." (Matthew 18:17)

Because some measures are complex, try to correct them and return them. Others may fail to escape their fleshly lust and return to live in their old worldly life. They will go back totally and expose themselves to the devil's attacks.

After separating from church, those who regret and repentant return, some correct themselves and start living new lives. The expectation is to return to church but not to be out of church. They might get spoilt by the enemy and remain there. For Christians, God is merciful and forgiving. His Word says whoever believes in Him shall be redeemed; He gave His begotten Son so that no one shall perish:

"For God so loved the world, that he gave his only begotten Son, that whosoever believeth in him should not perish, but have everlasting life." (John 3:16)

The church should also be careful not to affect such returning members according to the Word by not pushing them away and neglecting them, not unless the individual separates from the house of the Lord by his own jealous will by ignoring the advice and teachings given. Still, the person willing to return should be allowed the chance to return.

Church leaders with fatherly responsibility shall keep the herd with love and show the correct direction, not to fall short of the glory prepared for them as much as possible, with all they can. The church should upkeep each member by teaching the actual Word, teaching the true gospel, developing a strong faith foundation.

The church must make the effect for a continuous, healthy Christian-life teaching and attitude in members and follow up so that it can be visible enough to be witnessed and take care of the security of members as its primary issue. On the other hand, members' followers need to accept the effort made by the church to teach, be aware, and give spiritual support in the right way with goodwill and importance by taking it positively and with diligence. If such conditions prevail on both sides, it can be successful. Above all, it enables the church to serve its congregants to lead them in a way the glory of God is revealed in their life, increase in credit, and support those who need help and do the most honoured service to the Lord. What is more than this, seeing when God's recognition belongs to God?

23.3 To be covered by the grace of Christ

The objective of God is for us to resemble the image of Jesus. Romans 8:29, "For whom he did foreknow, he also did predestinate to be conformed to the idea of his Son, that he might be the firstborn among many brethren." We resemble Christ Jesus, including in our thinking. Philippians 2:5, "Let this mind be in you, which was also in Christ Jesus." Jesus has given us His example for us to follow Him in His earthly service. John 13:15, "For I have offered you an example, that ye should do as I have done to you."

The measurement for Christianity is living according to how Jesus lived on earth. 1 John 2:6, "He that saith he abideth in him also so to walk, even as he walked." Therefore, any teaching or preaching aims to help people live like Jesus. Colossians 1:28, "Whom we preach, warning every man, and teaching every man in all wisdom; that we may present every man perfect in Christ Jesus." As we are living on this earth, what challenges we may pass through, the objective is to make people resemble Christ.

A serviceman's important role would be to live like Jesus and be an example to others to live the same way. 1 Corinthians 11:1, "Be ye followers of me, even as I am of Christ. No glory equates to resembling Jesus on earth." This is a goal that we should pay any sacrifice to achieve. Philippians 3:8-9, "Yea doubtless, and I count all things but loss for the excellency of the knowledge of Christ Jesus my Lord: for whom I have suffered the loss of all things, and do count them but dung, that I may win Christ, And be found in him, not having my righteousness, which is of the law, but that which is through the faith of Christ, the righteousness which is of God by faith."

The secret to resembling Christ is in what Jesus told us, what we must do while living on earth in the right way, know it and understand it without vacillation, not mixing with any other way, living governed by Him, with righteousness and holiness. For this to happen, God will give a helper, His grace. For our weakness from the flesh, God will provide us the grace to the extent that amounts to as much as we need to withstand every day. But, of course, it happens based on our faith, not on knowledge or any personal power.

"Let us, therefore, come boldly unto the throne of grace, that we may obtain mercy, and find grace to help in time of need." (Hebrews 4:16)

Jesus the Nazarene, whose heart was humble, loves all men, He is compassionate, as it tells us in the Bible. To resemble Him, we shall be called and are selected so that we shall have His heart.

How we see people, accept, host, serve, understand, and love must be kept according to what Jesus commanded us.

"For who hath known the mind of the Lord, that he may instruct him? But we have the mind of Christ." (1 Corinthians 2:16)

"For even hereunto were ye called: because Christ also suffered for us, leaving us an example, that ye should follow his steps."   (1 Peter 2:21)

Noticing this message, we must follow as such. It requires a tremendous individual change of behaviour. It will not be productive if we cannot change ourselves and help ourselves with external pressure. Most of the time, accepting change forced by external power will not be satisfactory.

"Not a novice, lest being lifted with pride, he falls into the condemnation of the devil." (1 Timothy 3:6)

Resembling God resembles Jesus. Comparing Jesus thus means talking like He talked, doing what He did, frequent what He frequently does. Although we cannot be like someone we don't know, we can resemble Jesus if we don't know Him. Sometimes you say you know the person when you find someone singing, teaching, or doing something you recognise because you may know someone who has had a similar performance before. You may ask, who is this one who resembles so and so? Sometimes when someone sneezes, you may say, "This one seems like..." If that reminds you of someone you know, it means it has an issue.

It is through Christ Jesus that glorified to those partakers the eternal life among many brethren. We can only inherit this portion by resembling Jesus, not by personality.

CHAPTER 6

24. HOW SHALL WE AVOID HARMFUL PRACTICES AND THEIR RESULTS?

After earth came into being, the man reached the highest level through experience, research, and practice, especially innovation with his creative talents. As a result, we have the current status of civilisation.

We are using and seeing the best results of technology in thousands of years with the development of thousands of scientists' continuous efforts and sacrifices.

From the time Adam and Eve came into being, the life that started with socialisation among people and within their families, at the society level in an organised way, resulted in improvement by progressing from time to time to reach today's class. As a result, the population multiplied as commanded by God and filled the earth. Now billions of people are living in this world.

During these years of development, people in social, political, and economic (administrative) fields have changed and developed. Through these thousands of years, it is not only a good journey and beneficial change that has taken place but also the destruction of each other (war, robbery, internal and external conflict). Harmful and heavy damages have been happening to each other: big and destructive war, drought, problems, plague, disease, and warfare. On the contrary, development, and progress have also been recorded.

Human beings had to pass many destructions (plagues) due to disobedience as the years passed.

Human beings have developed a culture of leading their families and society to benefit all. Humans were able to have a cumulative effect through individual lives personally and as a society. Even family level in love, unity, thinking for each other, helping each other, in peace, consulting each other, living together in close ties to each other with social solid chains and assets. But, to benefit, on the contrary, those that put disadvantages and destructive practices also have adverse effects, particularly on uncivilised people in the form of culture and tradition.

Especially in concern to social assets, one mentioned is religion in different societies. However, we need not say anything about other types of faith here because this book focuses only on Christianity since it is one of them.

The Bible is the leading Christian book of teaching. It details how the human being developed socially and explains how man was dispersed all over the current world and how Christianity spread around this world. Christianity is part of the culture of society. Because of the birth of Christ, the religion took the name Christian from Christ. Christ existed in this world until He was grown and crucified to death because of His teaching. He was teaching the gospel and was crucified with no crime He committed. Jesus was preaching and teaching with divine power, defeating the devil. Then He went into His father's hug in Heaven and now exists. Jesus will be coming for the second time. Since Christianity got its name from Him, it doesn't require any other evidence (explanation) for its name other than this. So, Christianity is based on faith in the teachings of Jesus Christ's life.

However, there is one common saying based on the life the first disciples of Jesus lived and how disciples today live.

As the thinking goes, although Christianity complements culture and tradition, it is different in its content. Mainly, culture or tradition destroys its way. Those who believe in the dead ancestral spirit think they can receive instruction from ancestors; they may approach God and their ancestors (the nature of grandparents, grand-grandparents, and before them).

Does a dead person talk and help a human that is alive? No way! It, of course, is not difficult for anyone to understand that it is a mistake. But, with smartness, Satan can cheat people by imitating sounds like their parents and revealing them in spirit, and those who go through such practices and faith are mistaken. Satan is using them and is assigned to connect with them for such a purpose. They sacrifice blood or part of a body at least once a year for the spirit. The blood and body parts could be that of a human or animal. It is not difficult to imagine how wrong this type of practice is. The sacrifice of animal blood and flesh was a practice during the Old Testament, but because this was not good enough to clean man's sin, it was replaced in the New Testament's sacrifice through the blood of Jesus that cleanses once and for all.

"For when Moses had spoken every precept to all the people according to the law, he took the blood of calves and of goats, with water, and scarlet wool, and hyssop, and sprinkled both the book, and all the people, Saying, This is the blood of the testament which God hath enjoined unto you." (Blood of Jesus that cleanses once and for all; Hebrews 9:19-20)

"But if we walk in the light, as he is in the morning, we have fellowship one with another, and the blood of Jesus Christ his Son cleanseth us from all sin." (1 John 1:7)

"For it is not possible that the blood of bulls and of goats should take away sins." (Hebrews 10:4)

"But now in Christ Jesus ye who sometimes were far off are made nigh by the blood of Christ." (Ephesians 2:13)

"And I said unto him, Sir, thou knowest. And he said to me, These are they which came out of great tribulation, and have washed their robes, and made them white in the blood of the Lamb." (Revelation 7:14)

Jesus Christ has paid the price for our sins Himself as a Holy and clean sacrifice on the Cross of Calvary. Glory be to Jesus! The devil cannot set us free because he has missed his gift.

The damage that could happen is heavy on human beings (flesh, soul, and spirit). So, it is the witness for those people freed from the heart. Nevertheless, one who redeemed us through His blood is still present on the right side of His Father in Heaven, interceding for us.

Why should we expect a dead-defeated person to intercede for us instead of Christ? Why should we doubt this? It is from the deceiver, Satan. What people are confused about seems to differentiate between the Holy Spirit and the evil spirit. The Holy Spirit never leads anyone to such ridiculed and dirty things.

The Holy Spirit leads someone in a glorious and triumphant direction, as the Word says, written in the Bible. But, on the other hand, the evil spirit (Satan) leads to mischief, evildoing, sin, envy, hatred, murder, fornication, theft, lies, gossip, idol worship, witchcraft, spiritual illusion, and illuminist behaviours, to name a few. Hence, since there is a known evil spirit task, it is incredible why a man can't understand this. Therefore, what we can say is expressed in His words:

"For this people's heart is waxed gross, and their ears are dull of hearing, and their eyes they have closed; lest at any time they should see with their eyes, and hear with their ears, and should understand with their heart, and should be converted, and I should heal them." (Matthew 13:15)

Christianity is a path that takes you to Heaven, not hell. Therefore, Christianity must be free from harmful traditions, cultures, customs, and norms, absolutely. For example, some societies follow an annual event, worshipping and slaughtering /sacrificing an animal. When we look at this, it is not biblical at all.

This type of worship is called idol worship. It came from our forefathers and is a sacrifice to the dark spirit as Christians participate in such manners as sacrificing to the evil spirit. Therefore, to make family, friends, and neighbours happy to disappoint God and do something that will kindle His anger is a big mistake.

When we talk of harmful customs, religious (spiritual) views, or social interaction from the level of development we have reached, the technological advancement may not match. On the contrary, we shall not keep it going as far as the disadvantage is more significant because they stayed for long together. As far as it doesn't help us for our holiness and righteousness, we shall not follow it.

For the customs of the people are vain: for one cutteth a tree out of the forest, the work of the hands of the workman, with the axe. They deck it with silver and with gold; they fasten it with nails and with hammers, that it move not. They are upright as the palm tree, but speak not: they must needs be borne, because they cannot go. Be not afraid of them; for they cannot do evil, neither also is it in them to do good." (Jeremiah 10:3-5)

"Wherefore say unto the house of Israel, Thus saith the Lord God; Are ye polluted after the manner of your fathers? and commit ye whoredom after their abominations?" (Ezekiel 20:30)

Therefore, we shall shy away from such a way that doesn't make God happy. The way we administer, live, and worship shall not be what we inherited from traditions, culture, and worldly thinking, but only what has been told to us from God. What the Holy Spirit revealed to us and in a way that makes our God happy and glorifies him. Therefore, worldly law and order shall not separate us from our God.

CHAPTER 7

25. WHAT SHALL THE PEOPLE WHO BELIEVE IN THE EXISTENCE OF GOD DO?

God is jealous of His name and glory. He will take revenge if anyone stands to undermine His name or credit. We understand that such has happened to those we have read from the Bible. When He talked to the people of Israel through his servant Moses, He said this:

"Thou shalt not bow down thyself to them, nor serve them: for I the Lord thy God am a jealous God, visiting the iniquity of the fathers upon the children unto the third and fourth generation of them that hate me." (Exodus 20:5)

"Ye shall not go after other gods, of the gods of the people which are round about you; (For the Lord thy God is a jealous God among you) lest the anger of the Lord thy God be kindled against thee and destroy thee from off the face of the earth." (Deuteronomy 6:14-15)

"And Joshua said unto the people; Ye cannot serve the Lord: for he is a holy God; he is a jealous God; he will not forgive your transgressions nor your sins." (Joshua 24:19)

As indicated in the books above, God has indicated He is jealous. Therefore, what is expected of us and told to us is to listen, obey, and respect. Because if God is angry, He is sure no one can save us from His anger.

Thus, let us see the following points that happen from those people who are longing to see Him glorified.

26. CONCERNING HOLINESS

(as an individual, as a union, in a family)

After expelling the people of Israel from Egypt by using Moses, His servant, God had spoken to them about the temple. Holiness is His character and the primary behavioural exposure as written hereunder:

"For I am the Lord that bringeth you up out of the land of Egypt, to be your God: ye shall therefore be holy, for I am holy." (Leviticus 11:45)

Being holy to God is not a question to the congregation or group; it is everyone's issue. First, everyone should sanctify himself, then the whole assembly, the union, the family, generally all will be holy. The advantages of cleansing must be for an individual and the congregation. We shall be religious without considering time and space. People who follow the traditional way of worship might think that holiness is required when going to church only. Therefore, they only try to be holy (in fact, the physical body) when they go to church. Apart from having the capability of God to be present at all places simultaneously, He has declared that men (both male and female) are His temples. Therefore, God can be at any location and time with His people in His Spirit; thus, we shall be holy as far as we want to be with Him and care for Holiness.

26.1   As an individual

We are created uniquely in God's particular image and likeness and endowed with a unique appearance, stature, image, thinking power, colour, and body structure. Although we might have some similarities in parallel and size, the majority have a visible difference from each other.

It is not only in likeness and stature, but we can observe that we also are different in our behaviour. We can even keep children born to the same father and mother different from each other in many ways. As we approach our God, we come to Him to worship Him in Spirit; since the spirit is one, we shall be one also under this Spirit.

God the Father, God the Son, and God the Holy Spirit; three personalities, one God, in unison work together, we shall also be with one Spirit, heart, one thought shall be the worship to God when we are present in His temple.

The make of man is to be flesh, spirit, and soul, where these three entities operate with one accord without separation from the date of birth, though the creation of a person is different but must act as one in God's house. We shall serve the Lord by loving, cooperating, and accepting each other with one heart, thinking, and spirit.

The contribution of each and as a group to the service of God has great value. He understands this and contributes one's share with diligence, looking towards the Lord without focusing on anyone and serving without considering the type of sacrifices expected from everyone. Satan is always trying to make obstacles to the house of God and His people in different ways. Therefore, it is imperative to withstand the enemy's obstacles and continue without kneeling, standing without fail, and serving God's purpose. Christianity is a religion that requires great sacrifice. As far as we understand this, God has spoken in what condition He wants His people to serve Him as written in the Bible.

"And ye shall be holy unto me: for I the Lord am holy, and have severed you from other people, that ye should be mine." (Leviticus 20:26)

What God hates is sin, not the sinner. He doesn't want a man to be destroyed because of his sin since He is merciful. Particularly, He sent Jesus to earth and paid the sacrifice to pay the price for our sin to save a human being from eternal death. We are living in an era of mercy. We must be careful not to walk astray, thinking that we are left free to commit sin and continue to live that way. Then in this way, we might be kindling the wrath of God on ourselves.

When we do personal prayer or worship, we must make sure that God will hear and accept us and will answer to that for sure in faith. Because whatever response we get from Him is through our faith.

"Therefore I say unto you, What things soever ye desire, when ye pray, believe that ye receive them, and ye shall have them." (Mark 11:24)

Jesus spoke this, and the message is straightforward and clear. He said that whatever you prayed for, you shall receive, thus believe. It is impossible to translate it into something else or give any other explanation, but it should be as direct as it says with faith. Faith brings instant healing. We might have gotten so many prayer requests before the Lord. They could be answered prayers and not responded to ones. Especially to those who have not responded to prayers, we might not have asked the 'why' question. The problem is always from us; we must be sure that it is not from God because God does not have the problem of answering our questions. Let us see how a blind man questioned Jesus and received healing because of his faith:

"And Jesus said unto him, Go thy way; thy faith hath made thee whole. And immediately, he received his sight and followed Jesus in the way." (Mark 10:52)

This blind man believed that Jesus would heal him; Jesus also saw his faith and said to the man, "Your faith has enabled you to cure," and he instantly was healed and walked seeing.

We shall receive or inherit what we have prayed for in such a faith. However, the response we get when we pray earnestly and ordinarily differs from each other. We can give witness to this even today.

Apart from this, the other important thing is that it needs our righteousness. Holiness is essential to receive a response to our prayer. We cannot make God happy without approaching Him in the right way. Sin is something that keeps our God away from us. God cannot present himself because His Holiness will not allow Him wherever sin is. Therefore, individually, we must try to sanctify ourselves to our God by obeying Him and living righteously and in such a way before Him. Then, we can work and be named holy when we have righteousness.

If everyone keeps himself holy, then God will bless everyone. When this happens, the glory of God will come upon the congregation. It will be an excellent visitation time. We need to know that even if most people cannot stand for the glory of God, He will always have someone that sanctifies for Him. Of course, we shall not be comforted by this, but we shall individually try our best to be blessed more than ever.

26.2   As a union

God wants to see His people be in a union. The word from the Psalms of David says this:

"Behold, how good and how pleasant it is for brethren to dwell together in unity!" (Psalm 133:1)

The people of God come together for a great purpose. Therefore, the gathering in the house of God shall not be like an ordinary house gathering. On the contrary, the very reason the people of God gather in a place is for the primary purpose of worshipping the Lord, believing Him, blessing Him, and receiving blessings from Him (healing, mercy, solution for the problems.)

God will hear prayers, of course. Where the congregation rebukes evil spirits, the evil cannot work. But, bondage will break, and prophesy and revelation will start working. Generally, God will confirm His visitation in such a manner.

Things that will not happen during private prayer will occur when the people of God are together. Not being among the congregation will cause us to miss what God does amongst the community.

Today, because of the technological advancement man has reached, many people like to attend seated and watching from home through TV and online transmissions of YouTube and other facilities. As a result, we have reached a stage where people prefer not to attend church.

It is done because of people's will to absent themselves individually and physically from what God wants us to do, but knowingly or unknowingly, disobeying the Word and focusing more on personal feelings, losing interest in coming to church becomes a problem from time to time.

Likewise, when their faith in Christ is lost, some have gone to the extent of worshipping Satan as their god and made a way of faith, and doing it is becoming secret to the public. After going his own way when he departed from the Lord, he cannot imagine what happened. This type of person will have a much shorter time for Satan to control than it took to put him under the power of the Lord. So, this is pronounced in the life of many people today, those who step back.

Coming to churches can be a problem because of some unfavourable situations. A man could have many disappointments. But it shall not be a reason not to go to church because the church belongs to God, not any human being on earth. Discussing with the responsible person in a brotherly manner may be required. We should search for a solution even if it is challenging. Try to become a crown winner and victorious in that. It will bring a chance to make the Lord happy. But because many believers consider such thoughts foolish, we see them as separate from unity. So, it is an honest mistake when we check it against the Word.

Today, more than ever, we have reached a stage where the enemy is highly struggling day and night openly on this issue in the house of the Lord. For this, Christians, on the contrary, need to be strong individually and as a group to fight them back. We should understand that fighting the enemy in unity gives us much stronger power than battling separately. We should know that following what God loves and prefers is more significant than anything; one should notice there is nothing better than this for one who likes to worship and obey his God. Seeking any other alternative to separate himself from the unity of God's people is a lack of consciousness, but there is no unity which the enemy does not fight or where you do not see human weakness.

If the enemy is not fighting the union, either that union is living agreeing with the enemy or might have faced an intense fight from the enemy and is living a victorious life overcoming the enemy's conflict. It does not mean that a victorious congregation doesn't face any challenge from the enemy. It is known because Satan will not stop fighting until the last time the Lord throws him into deep prison. Therefore, it is not right that people go from one church to another, thinking that one is better. But the correct way is to stay in the same congregation by praying, advising, giving service, and trying to push towards its glory and work together, stimulating and supporting each other; doing this would indeed glorify God, and He likes to be glorified.

"And they continued steadfastly in the apostles' doctrine and fellowship, and in breaking of bread, and in prayers." (Acts 2:42)

As indicated above, we read that Apostles were respected when they ate in their service and union. The Word teaches us that we also need to be vigilant for such. What we use now in this time is the opposite of this. Each person considers himself capable and better than his friend, thinking wiser and thinking deeply; thus, whoever accepts any advice from another one is very rare. This way, making God happy would be a big mistake. If we could follow the Apostles' example, it would be profitable and help us defeat the enemy, and we cannot doubt.

26.3   At home (as family)

The foundation of the church is home. People living in a family are husband and wife, children, and others who live with them. It means it is a place where people less than a church life are the first union where people of God live together. The minimum number of people in a family starts from two. When every family becomes intense, the church also becomes firm, but under some circumstances, if the church weakens, the problem can go so far as affecting the church and to the extent of making the church also weak. Therefore, the church should take care of both the individual and the church.

"For this cause left I thee in Crete, that thou shouldest set in order the things that are wanting, and ordain elders in every city, as I had appointed thee: If any be blameless, the husband of one wife, having faithful children not accused of riot or unruly. For a bishop must be blameless, as the steward of God; not self-willed, not soon angry, not given to wine, no striker, not given to filthy lucre; But a lover of hospitality, a lover of good men, sober, just, holy, temperate." (Titus 1:5-8)

The behaviour of individuals can happen by people living within the home more than by anyone outside. It is true, everyone knows. We hear much information from many people of God, they are witnesses in this era. It indicates that people would like to express their internal ideas freely in their family rather than publicly or in a congregation. This is only possible if it is external feelings, not core feelings; otherwise, only saying what they think will give them acceptance.

Christians should show the same character anywhere (at home or outside). So, he who shows double standards is Satan because he is a liar. We must notice that it does not mean those whose feelings change are under Satan's influence. But those people who do not control themselves and do not obey the Word show similar behaviour. Therefore, we need to be careful because such behaviour is not supposed to be ours, not for Christians, and we shall not practice it since it will make us fall in danger and expose us to the enemy. So, we need to be careful. Lord Himself spoke about this in His words.

"Verily, verily, I say unto you, He that entereth not by the door into the sheepfold, but climbeth up some other way, the same is a thief and a robber." (John 10:1)

This person who is a thief or a robber is Satan. We should not inherit the behaviour of Satan, but we are nominated to inherit that of the Lord. We will enter through the right door, on the straight road through Christ. Our leader and teacher is Christ, who is Jesus. We cannot take anybody as our leader; our leader is the only one with no fault found and doesn't have any weaknesses, Christ Jesus. Consider that exceptional if a man doesn't make mistakes and is perfect. We shall make Jesus above us and excellent in his moral authority above all in our heart, which will help us during problems so that we shall not kneel to situations. When we see back on the Lord, it will give us strength to not fall into temptations. Jesus never tried to make people happy. To use the word tells us where we should put our focus.

"Wherefore seeing we also are compassed about with so great a cloud of witnesses, let us lay aside every weight, and the sin which doth so easily beset us, and let us run with patience the race that is set before us, Looking unto Jesus the author and finisher of our faith; who for the joy that was set before him endured the cross, despising the shame, and is set down at the right hand of the throne of God." (Hebrews 12:1-2)

We should look toward the fulfiller and accomplisher of our faith, Jesus, as explained in the word above. To those who believe in Christ Jesus, since He is the head of our home, we need to authorise Him to be head and show that in practice.

When Jesus becomes head of our home, if anything goes wrong, this Lord will take care to correct the spoilt; moreover, His glory, blessings, the favour will be plenty in our home. When our house becomes a living place glorified, it will be a blessing and a solid foundation for the church. In holiness, we can make the Lord head of our home, not without, because Lord cannot be present where there is no holiness. Therefore, we should be separated and made holy if we want the Lord to be present in our house. We will find our issues accomplished when we split and get holy because we will receive help from Him and His mercy.

When a sanctified family comes to church, the whole congregation becomes sanctified, then the glory of God begins to be revealed, and miracles and wonders will happen amidst the assembly. The people of God will then be partakers of this situation. No doubt that the devil will start to test us when the glory of God begins to come among us.

To withstand the devil's attempt, we must dress in the weapons of warfare and be prepared to fight. The enemy fights externally and prefers to use those convenient to him internally and selects deploys. Christian believers need to know this, be ready not to be cheated easily, and be aware of the devil's evil work.

In this era, many believers face this type of attack. They have become causes for the church's weakness and even demolish it, exposing it to being attacked by opposing bodies and creating antagonistic groups. God has spoken openly in His words, saying:

"Now I beseech you, brethren, by the name of our Lord Jesus Christ, that ye all speak the same thing, and that there be no divisions among you; but that ye be perfectly joined together in the same mind and in the same judgment." (1 Corinthians 1:10)

"For our comely parts have no need: but God hath tempered the body together, having given more abundant honour to that part which lacked: That there should be no schism in the body; but that the members should have the same care one for another." (1 Corinthians 12:24-25)

"Idolatry, witchcraft, hatred, variance, emulations, wrath, strife, seditions, heresies..." (Galatians 5:20)

"A man that is a heretic after the first and second admonition reject; Knowing that he that is such is subverted, and sinneth, being condemned of himself." (Titus 3:10-11)

The abovementioned verses explain that separation is wrong and not allowed among Christians. One way or the other, a man exposes himself to unworthy or some mistaken issue. It is an obvious truth that people make a mistake knowingly or unknowingly. Some people do not accept opportunities given to them, blinding their eyes. They prefer providing their justification when compared to the word leading themselves with their thoughts and guiding, giving it a priority, and selecting their way.

Because God is not taking immediate action, they make mistakes considering it is allowed for them to keep making the same mistake, thus they do not get the chance of mercy to correct and return. For those who produce, God is merciful. He will forgive them, but many people undermine this great mercy from God and continue practicing their mistakes, which is wrong; therefore, they need to stop and question themselves. It has made them reluctant and caused them to fail to return.

Stubbornness, conflict, break-up, hatred, gossip, envy, and bad ideas come from the enemy devil but not from the Holy Spirit, without a doubt. But, on the contrary, it can be that peace, unity, generosity, blessings, constructive rebuke, and helping each other are all from Holy Spirit. But, if you notice, there is a significant difference between the two.

Even though people know the difference between the two, instead of following God's will and doing according to the Word, they do whatever they feel is right and miss the correct direction. Some even twist the meaning written in the Word and give it a traversed sense and are found in a twisted manner and continue with their mistaken feeling.

Marriages end with divorce because of the mistakes taken wrongly; the problem going up to this might also affect the church and society. The church's peace is affected when a family is not in harmony. It must be clear.

The problem will not stop at one point in our life journey; it might affect others. Instead of God, we might end up damaging our relationship with God and make Satan happy by doing something terrible; we must be careful. If we don't do this, we might be like the donkey in the parable often shared in my culture, "let the grass never grow once I am dead," not caring for others, yet we will be receiving punishment for the wrong we did with eternal death; this is not something difficult not to imagine.

<u>We need to return to God</u>. We should quickly return to the correct direction; therefore, as the Word says, we shall live in love, peace, unity, understanding, acceptance, and concern. To the same extent, the devil is strengthening his fight. A Christian passing through tempting situations may not easily defeat the devil. Indeed, the enemy fights every Christian.

"Blessed is the man that endureth temptation: for when he is tried, he shall receive the crown of life, which the Lord hath promised to them that love him." (James 1:12)

One who likes to receive his crown from the Lord when temptation comes from the enemy must ensure he is sure to endure it and stand firm to fight with the devil courageously without giving up. Then that will enable him to start seeing God's glory.

27. ONE HEART, IDEA, AND SPIRIT

When Lord Jesus was on this earth, He gave so many heavenly hopes to His disciples. One which was a terrific promise He passed and was accomplished a few days after His resurrection was the reception of the Holy Spirit while the Apostles were seated together.

"And when the day of Pentecost was fully come, they were all with one accord in one place. And suddenly there came a sound from heaven as of a rushing mighty wind, and it filled all the house where they were sitting. And there appeared unto them cloven tongues like as of fire, and it sat upon each of them. And they were all filled with the Holy Ghost, and began to speak with other tongues, as the Spirit gave them utterance." (Acts 2:1-4)

It happened as He has told them of the hope, and the hope given was saying this:

"If ye love me, keep my commandments. And I will pray for the Father, and he shall give you another Comforter, that he may abide with you forever." (John 14:15-15)

"But the Comforter, which is the Holy Ghost, whom the Father will send in my name, he shall teach you all things, and bring all things to your remembrance, whatsoever I have said unto you." (John 14:26)

A man can tell a lie that may not be known or detected immediately. But God can examine the heart and kidney, making it difficult to lie to Him. If one thinks of lying to

God, one will be cheating himself, but it is impossible to lie to God. Man can see the face but can't see the heart.

"And I will kill her children with death; and all the churches shall know that I am he which searcheth the reins and hearts: and I will give unto every one of you according to your works." (Revelation 2:23)

Not only does God know the heart and kidney, but it tells us that He can also read our minds because He is the one who created us, and this can pay us our price according to our work because He has all the details precisely before Him about every person on earth. Therefore, to receive our values respectfully, knowing this, living before Him with righteousness, and being obedient enables us to obtain the crown from Him undoubtedly. If we don't understand this and live, it feels good to us, but if death comes suddenly, the way we live is known to God, who knows our everyday life before Him and will reward us accordingly. Above all, discomforting someone's heart will not make God happy. That is why if you know someone who has a grievance against you, you must go in advance and reconcile with your friend before you kneel to pray. It should be explained in the Word as follows:

"Therefore if thou bring thy gift to the altar, and there rememberest that thy brother hath ought against thee; Leave there thy gift before the altar, and go thy way; first be reconciled to thy brother, and then come and offer thy gift." (Matthew 5:23-24)

How many of us read this word and implement it accordingly? There is a difference between knowing and practicing the talk. As the Bible says, a word separated from faith has no value. Therefore, we must try hard not to separate our faith from the word written in the Bible.

"For the customs of the people are vain: for one cutteth a tree out of the forest, the work of the hands of the workman, with the axe. They deck it with silver and with gold; they fasten it with nails and with hammers, that it move not. They are upright as the palm tree but speak not: they must be borne because they cannot go. Therefore, be not afraid of them, for they cannot do evil, and neither is it in them to do good." (Jeremiah 10:3-5)

"Wherefore say unto the house of Israel, Thus saith the Lord God; Are ye polluted after the manner of your fathers? And commit ye whoredom after their abominations?" (Ezekiel 20:30)

Hence, we need to avoid such an unpleasant situation with God. The way we obey, live, and worship not on what we have inherited from tradition, culture, but follow what God spoke to us, what the Holy Spirit revealed to us, making our God happy and glorified. The written law and order shall not separate us from the words of our God.

28. TO BE THIRSTY, TO BE FILLED WITH THE HOLY SPIRIT

When anyone accepts the Lord as his personal Saviour, the Holy Spirit begins working with new converts immediately. The power in us, which died because of Adam's sin is revitalised and restored to life by Christ's control, for the breath God put when God created Adam first through our nostrils is still in us. It confirms that He has appeared in various ways in those who have accepted the Lord.

Depending on the individual's spiritual readiness and arrangements for faith, it may take days, weeks, months, or years for the Holy Spirit to manifest its preciousness in life. For example: as a believer who has accepted the Lord, he can obtain unique tongues, prophesying, see visions and revealings. Not that one person receives all graces, but that God, who can see the believers' capacities at the time, will give him what he can bear and with what the person trusted can take part to the advantage of the people He has selected. Those who choose to continue in union with the Lord will soon begin to see the fruit of the Holy Ghost in their lives. Serve the Lord with the grace and anointing of their gifts, and the Lord will move them from glory to glory, for the Lord is faithful to his word.

"And it shall come to pass afterward, that I will pour out my spirit upon all flesh; and your sons and your daughters shall prophesy, your old men shall dream dreams, your young men shall see visions." (Joel 2:28)

This prophecy was going on throughout the two millenniums. As soon as the borne again accepts Jesus, they will receive the Holy Spirit. In devotion, one needs to reveal this incident in life and strive to keep the fire burning and work for life. The presence of the Holy Spirit has the word and helps the righteous life of the believer.

Suddenly, if the believer falls into sin, the Holy Spirit will abandon his presence, for he cannot walk with sin. If the believers realise that the Holy Spirit has left him because of his sin, they should repent and invite it back. If he repents with genuine return, the Holy Spirit will return and begin to help the faithful person's journey through life as long as he remains loyal and sanctified and works as before. It requires an exceptional understanding. While some may have tried and failed to recognise the power of the Holy Ghost in their lives, they may or may not have wanted to believe in the same Holy Spirit that preceded their ministry.

To receive the fullness of the Holy Spirit, we need to constantly have the thirst and earnestness to be filled with the Spirit to escape the temptations of the flesh because the flesh may mislead us into temptation. The Holy Spirit's fire must constantly burn so that we can break the devil's trap within us.

We need to be filled with the Holy Spirit all the time. So, every time we ask, we are filled with the Holy Spirit; it can change to a new one from when we received it at the beginning. That's why we see many believers having better and more graceful service in the later stage of their life than they used to be at the beginning. But, of course, their journey did not mean that it was smooth; they may pass through many trials, ups and downs and pass through forced labour, and many other tests. There is no doubt that they may have lost hope because the enemy attempts to think of any weapon and tactic that he can to defeat the person. So, the Holy Spirit, in the process, may not depart as far as the person doesn't lose hope. The Lord will fight for us and oppose what stands against us, saying, I will not let him down that have come to me.

"But the Lord is faithful, who shall establish you, and keep you from evil." (2 Thessalonians 3:3)

We are more than winners, not in our strength and power, but in the grace that the Lord gives us. Therefore, we need to always fall under the Lord's feet to put our problems before His throne and to keep awake, gently praying, with the whole spirit, covered with undeserved kindness, and vigilant to do His will. He will protect us from enemy arrows when we can meet this situation because His protection is constantly around us.

We need to know how much damage we can have if we do not have the protection and guard from the Lord, as the enemy runs to destroy us night and day. Problems arise when we give in to weakness in the flesh and open the door to the enemy, and when we lack the protection of our God, the enemy quickly tries to take control of everything.

When we are thirsty and filled with the Holy Spirit, our hope becomes a reality, and we will have a spiritual understanding in which we can break down the enemy's work. We praise the Holy Spirit in our ministry. And we will have the opportunity to do God's will and thoughts. Being filled with the spirit is not merely a result of our genuine desire from the heart and a manifestation of what we receive as we faithfully apply it to His glory, and it grows ever more and more. God is not a man; He will not allow the devil to work throughout our time.

CHAPTER 8

29. HOW FAR DO WE BELIEVE IN THE WORD OF GOD?

In life, or at work, in our going out and coming in, we should follow in our life journey the four gospels and the messages from the Apostles, which is the good news. This will place us in the correct position, we need that for us. We shall not compromise today's good work for tomorrow's bad jobs in Christianity. That is why in Christianity, a life that we lived yesterday will not be a guarantee for today. That is why Christianity took everyday life as a measuring tool. Comfort and delight will not be what we will have in the world but suffering, as the Lord told in His words.

"These things I have spoken unto you, that in me ye might have peace. In the world ye shall have tribulation: but be of good cheer; I have overcome the world." (John 16:33)

We shall not be hopeless with this because of what we read in the above verse; he said, "don't worry, I have won the world." Therefore, we shall not feel stressed about it. But, of course, the problem, the test, the suffering, the pain, the harassment, the famine, the lack, the nakedness, and the disease will push us to the extent of disliking living on earth. But this suffering, compared to the crown we get in the heavenly realm, cannot be equated to and cannot distract us from getting the highest privilege.

As far as we read and know the Word in our earthly life, these things may test our inner being (spirituality) to pass through such a situation; we shall strengthen our inner being and be prepared to die with victory. But, as the Lord spoke, if we can be determined and decisive, agree with Him becoming strong, agree with Him, stand firm, He is loyal and will not hand us over to the enemy because He will help us with His grace and remain faithful.

Nobody wants to receive suffering, of course. It cannot be an option to receive suffering. We cannot accept suffering when we are supposed to. However, because of Adam and Eve's sin, whatever was said to them has reached us, passing from generation to generation. This generational curse and evil can disappear by the payment made by Jesus Christ's suffering and death. We are made accessible. However, the flesh is living under defeat; today, the defeated devil is testing those who forgot the word or didn't know, suppressing them. Therefore, he doesn't choose those Christians who see the word and stand firm on the word. The word says the following to destroy the devil:

"Above all, taking the shield of faith, wherewith ye shall be able to quench all the fiery darts of the wicked." (Ephesians 6:16)

We need to grow in resemblance to the Lord until it is visible among people that we love. It is difficult for those of us who are walking in the flesh. Hence, this should not distract us from growing and resembling the Lord. Above all, the Lord wants His love to be magnificently visible in our lives. The Lord has openly spoken that it would need great sacrifice.

"For if ye love them which love you, what reward have ye? do not even the publicans the same?" (Matthew 5:46)

Again, about loving each other, the Word says this:

"And above all things have fervent charity among your-selves: for charity shall cover the multitude of sins." (1 Peter 4:8)

If we can't love every man, how can we be deployed to save the unsaved ones? If we do not love each other and go out to save others, we will face a significant problem. The problem will be because we are not operating with one heart, idea, and spirit to work with understanding and misunderstanding. It will hinder our salvation work and open doors for problems. It requires convincing the believer to come to God in eternal hope through love, patience, witness, and persuasion. After witnessing those willing to accept the Lord to make them strong in their faith, we should have a conducive situation to provide them with a continuous biblical study lesson. They not only learn the Word but also become strong in their faith. They must take water baptism as the Lord ordered. They ultimately need ongoing follow-up and help to be strong in their faith until such. We shall do all that has been done to us when we received the Lord the first time.

God is not a human being. We can never cheat Him in any other way. We must fulfil what we read to perform in our life journey and not take the devil's advice.

We have no choice except to avoid sin and practice this in our lives. It is fooling oneself and doesn't work to contrast it to the current situation and say this doesn't work this time, but it is an old way. Since God made everything through the time when He created all the world, He knows when and where things happened as early as He made and knows today and even what will happen in the future until the end of the world. Hence, living according to the Word is the only option.

We should live knowing that, and we shall not be obedient to the world and resemble it knowing this in all our walks of life. When He returns the second time, He wants to find us where He kept us. But if we leave our place, we will be misleading our creator. It will be a significant loss. Mainly what we read in His words will be missed; thus, we shall declare to work on us and declare on us to work and practice it visibly and put effort as written as follows:

- I am a new creation = "Therefore if any man is in Christ, he is a new creature: old things are passed away; behold, all things become new." (2 Corinthians 5:17)
- I am more than a conqueror = Romans 8:37, "Nay, we are more than conquerors through him that loved us in all these things." (Romans 8:37)
- I am blessed = "Blessed be the God and Father of our Lord Jesus Christ, who hath blessed us with all

spiritual blessings in heavenly places in Christ..."
(Ephesians 1:3)

- Victory is mine = "But thanks be to God, which giveth us the victory through our Lord Jesus Christ." (1 Corinthians 15:57)
- I am the light of the world = "Ye are the light of the world. A city that is set on a hill cannot be hidden." (Matthew 5:14)
- I am born again from an indestructible seed = "Being born again, not of corruptible seed, but of incorruptible, by the word of God, which liveth and abideth forever." (1 Pet 1:23)
- I am not sinful because I believed in Jesus Christ = "There is, therefore, no condemnation to them which are in Christ Jesus, who walk not after the flesh but after the Spirit." (Romans 8:1)
- You become healed with His strip = "Who himself bare our sins in His own body on the tree, that we, being dead to sins, should be sealed." (1 Peter 2:24)
- I am given power over all evil spirits = "Live unto righteousness: by whose stripes ye were he. Behold, I give unto you the ability to tread on serpents and scorpions, and over all the power of the enemy: and nothing shall by any means hurt you." (Luke 10:19)
- What I bind on earth will be bound in Heaven because I have Heaven's key = "And I will give unto thee the keys of the kingdom of heaven: and whatsoever thou shalt bind on earth shall be bound in heaven: and whatsoever thou shalt loose on earth shall be loosed in heaven." (Matthew 16:19)

Many other words of God cover us with power in the Bible. Thus, we must know these, produce the required capacity, and walk in faith.

The glory of God's will starts to operate in us when we accept these and other words that give us power (declare it on ourselves). Then, we can live on earth like an authority, work, and provide instruction. It will be a surprise even to people who have known us until they admire the glory revealed to us.

The Lord needs to govern our life. We want the Lord to be seen in our life as far as we have the passion in us. He will do it because He has promised us, except in one condition, if we fail to be sanctified and cannot walk holy, and when His love and faith could not be visible in us, we can't glorify Him. God will not operate where there is no holiness and sanctity.

"And ye shall be holy unto me: for I the Lord am holy, and have severed you from other people, that ye should be mine." (Leviticus 20:26)

"For thou art a holy people unto the Lord thy God: the Lord thy God hath chosen thee to be a special people unto himself, above all people that are upon the face of the earth." (Deuteronomy 7:6)

If we say we are separated from this Holy God when He says be holy, we can only approach Him by being holy. No other way is allowed, not permitted. It is a mistake to consider Him unknowing, not allowed. It is a mistake to argue about something that is not allowed and a sin. It is a problem for many people with whom are we arguing when He has already said you can only approach me this way. Since He is a merciful God, He will accept and return us.

People sacrifice for something they believe, whether it is right or wrong. It doesn't matter whether it is a heavenly or earthly organisation. They are determined to sacrifice as far as it needs them to succeed; they will be struggling for it to the end.

On the contrary, God's people become negligent in doing the heavenly hopeful thing. Which one is better? Is it earthly or heavenly? It will help us notice each other's movements carefully, but the weakness of being human limits us. But we should know and prepare ourselves and keep diligently under the will of God.

However, we shall believe the Holy Book is for us, and we shall use it in a holy and sanctified manner; we shall have the true love which in us be displayed in Lord's time and start serving with it. Due to this, the anointing will advance strengthening, and we shall begin observing miracles and wonders in our lives. It is not a dream we are talking about but practically and objectively taking place on those who believe in those who have faith in God. Nothing moves God except a faithful approach. He has never failed those who trusted Him. We receive God's power through trusting Him. Whatever happens to us is based on the level of our faith.

"And, behold, a woman of Canaan came out of the same coasts, and cried unto him, saying, Have mercy on me, O Lord, thou Son of David; my daughter is grievously vexed with a devil. But he answered her not a word. And his disciples came and besought him, saying, Send her away; for she crieth after us. But he answered and said, I am not sent but unto the lost sheep of the house of Israel. Then came she and worshipped him, saying, Lord, help me. But he answered and said, It is not meet to take the children's bread and to cast it to dogs. And she said, Truth, Lord: yet the dogs eat of the crumbs which fall from their masters' table. Then Jesus answered and said unto her, woman, great is thy faith: be it unto thee even as thou wilt. And her daughter was made whole from that very hour." (Matthew 15:22-28)

We must understand that whatever we pray, if we do not get an answer from God, the problem is not from the giver (God) but due to a lack of faith.

"And the apostles said unto the Lord, Increase our faith. And the Lord said, If ye had faith as a grain of mustard seed, ye might say unto this sycamine tree, Be thou plucked up by the root, and be thou planted in the sea, and it should obey you. But which of you, having a servant plowing or feeding cattle, will say unto him by and by, when he has come from the field, Go and sit down to meat?" (Luke 17:5-7)

Faith is a decisive issue. Without faith, it is not possible to talk with God. Without faith, it is not possible to accept God. Without faith, it is impossible to succeed in working with God. Generally, God is not happy without faith. Hebrews 11:6, "But without faith it is impossible to please him: for he that cometh to God must believe that he is and that he is a rewarder of them that diligently seek him." Jesus did not answer directly to the question, "please add us more faith." Instead Jesus, for the query, "adds us faith," did not say, "I will add you faith," even though he understood the importance of the question but instead the answer Jesus gave was to test what they did with the faith which He had already gave them.

Therefore, before we present ourselves before God for prayer, we better check ourselves and approach Him faithfully. What we should make sure of in our faith is that He is Almighty, faithful, miracle worker, victorious, merciful, forgiving, loving, unlimited blessing. And equally to those who go outside His will, He provides His will. Those who disrespect Him, who are sinking in their fleshly lust, those who have a lousy heart, those who do not have the word, those disobey, are those God will punish. We shall understand that He is jealous of His glory; we need to fear Him, respect, obey, and tremble before Him.

Our life should not be foolish, like a person going to market and returning home, if we do not provide our life the proper direction to walk, giving it the appropriate respect, it means that we are not thinking about our everlasting place. As the Lord spoke:

"For what is a man advantaged, if he gain the whole world, and lose himself, or be cast away?" (Luke 9:25)

Therefore, not to remain short of eternal life, we shall neglect the world and its benefits and hold on to the highest, eternal life. The Lord came to earth to save us from eternal death. Thus, we must know that if we don't live understanding why He sacrificed Himself for us and remain obedient to worldly life, we must know that we are damaging all that He paid for us.

If we fall in such a way, we shall notice that this will result in a judgement that will throw us into everlasting fire. No one can mock God's name. The main thing the Lord Jesus wants to happen for us is saving our souls from falling into hell. He kept us from a price He paid to a sacrifice that no wealth can buy by defeating the devil. Those who did not understand this outstanding achievement are unlucky weak ones.

CHAPTER 9

30. LET US CHECK OURSELVES THROUGH OUR SERVICE

Once a person has received Jesus Christ as his Saviour, he must next prepare himself for service. Finally, a saved person should accept the church's service to contribute to others; we must show as much diligence as possible.

The service we give and do are all for the sake of the Lord; thus, whatever we serve should be for a cause serving the Lord. You will always find mistakes and some distractions from every human being. If those who are our leaders, for some reason, make a mistake that will disappoint us, that hurts our feeling. If they do something questionable or disappointing, we shall be careful not to be distracted and stop our service to the Lord because of the mistake done by these people because our service is to the Lord, not to those individuals. We instead must pray for the people who created the problem. The Lord knows how to do it wonderfully and will make us effective by giving it to Him to correct it. He will solve it smoothly instead of struggling with it and give us a relaxed spirit to make us successful. The exemplary performance we display in this way will teach those who serve us.

Service we give to God should be with honesty and humility lowering ourselves to God and His people, fulfilling the Heavenly will (2 Timothy 4:70). Service giving, therefore, is thinking that instead of standing for our advantage, benefit people and glorify God. If this is what we understand as servants, that this is the right way, a service person should keep himself holy, give his will to the Lord, and know why he creates the need to worship God (being subjugated). We should understand that service delivered through the Holy Spirit depends on faith and grace. According to the Word, the objective is to serve the Lord and develop trust and assistance. It must rely on willingness and voluntarism, obliged with the love of the Lord.

However, one of the problems we might face may not be possible to resist the power of the flesh, which can be testing hard. Therefore, standing firm by asking the help of the Lord must try to come out of the testing situation with no problem, without missing anything, and we may continue serving the Lord.

"For this thing I besought the Lord thrice, that it might depart from me. And he said unto me, My grace is sufficient for thee: my strength is made perfect in weakness. I will most gladly, therefore, rather glory in my infirmities, that the power of Christ may rest upon me." (2 Corinthians 12:8-9)

Because of the challenges they face, some of these services fail to withstand and have patience; they quit the service they give, may refrain from continuing to offer their service, and eventually stop.

It is essential to sit down and think about how this action will help or harm. Being spontaneous and losing hope is not expected from a Christian. Since being spontaneous has dangers, it is better to walk patiently and collected, enabling a long journey without a problem. Because rushing can usually cover up thinking, it may not give a chance to know the important from the harmful and may not give time and expose to danger. One who pays the price for our effort is the Lord, and one whom we are serving is Him; then our faithfulness shall be to Him only. His word about the service says the following:

"And in every work that he began in the service of the house of God, and in the law, and in the commandments, to seek his God, he did it with all his heart, and prospered." (2 Chronicles 31:21)

When we receive Jesus Christ as our Saviour, we receive service simultaneously. We are obliged to give the service we receive with a reasonable response. Because if we want to receive the crown of victory, this is the only gate. To look into any short path would be a matter of superficial scar developing but with no results. The Lord is righteous in His judgement. Honest to His words. He is jealous of His glory and name. Therefore, we shall make sure we are fulfilling our obligatory will.

"And they set the priests in their divisions, and the Levites in their courses, for the service of God, which is at Jerusalem; as it is written in the book of Moses." (Ezra 6:18)

Services that are in one local church

There are many different services in a church. Every church's service type can differ depending on the progress it has made, and it does not mean all the services need to be present in every church.

Among the service types, the most known are pastors, elders, evangelists, prophets, deacons, apostles, teachers, and singers. Others include gospel witness groups, program leaders, children's teachers, counsellors, administrators, accountants, secretaries, messengers, security guards, mentors, drivers, etc. We may find such and many more services in a church.

Most of those assigned to these service types could be church members. They can offer services paid on a wage basis or free service with no payment. Some churches have employed workers on a salary basis.

Those with a large congregation and high income can have employed workers with paid professional staff. But elders are appointed and designated. Elders must evaluate the nominees for the other service types they elected based on the members' information. Witnesses from members should be assigned accordingly when such an assignment is given by consulting members, receiving critics, and assessing the witnesses of members' findings. When someone offers a job to such people, it depends on the person's anointing. Those who do not have any other income from any other source will be given some support from the church to help them serve and meet their fleshly needs but may not equate salary in the house of the Lord; no service is of greater importance than any other service. Every service is considered respectful, essential, and necessary for the home of the Lord. It is significant; therefore, with whatever we can, what is in us, what we prepare for, or what church will deploy us to service, we shall be serving with complete willingness, which will be respected. When we ask the following questions, we can check how far we have contributed to the service.

How do we know what type of service anointing we have in us?

Your call is for the service of God. In the growing process, you might have thought of those called missionaries, pastors, evangelists, and full-time servants of the church. But the Bible tells us the calling of every Christian for service (as we find in Ephesians 4:4; Romans 1:6-7). Being called for salvation includes service calls also. They are the same. Whatever you do, you are called a full-time Christian service giver. Whether you are assigned for a service or willingly cooperating for any service in the church, whatever you do is a service. We get from the Lord who weighs and values our pay accordingly and we will succeed. I believe that a Christian who is not serving contradicts this point of view.

When God created every person, He had unique talents, gifts, and anointing. So, it becomes visible once these people come to Jesus with the help of the Holy Spirit.

Service starts in the brain. To be a service person requires a change of thinking. God focuses mainly on what we perform and why we do it.

Above all, when we apply our will to serve the Lord, successful people admire us. But on the other hand, if the Holy Spirit reveals whatever we were hiding in ourselves, knowingly or unknowingly, it can be revealed through revelation (prophecy) and there we should accept with faith. In this way or another, whatever potential is in us when indicated, we must know that we must give that service without complaint. Whatever we involve, if we see results after a successful service and it benefits some people, we shall continue with that, not imitate another person's service, which others have shown success with just because they succeeded. We know our gift from the achievement we get when we serve but not because we know it and follow suit, and later, if we fail, it will be a waste of energy and a lack of self-awareness. Therefore, we should help where we know and understand to serve, and something we are anointed with but not just follow and serve because other people were appreciated and became successful with it.

"Having then gifts differing according to the grace that is given to us, whether prophecy, let us prophesy according to the proportion of faith." (Romans 12:6)

"Now there are diversities of gifts, but the same Spirit. And there are differences of administrations, but the same Lord. And there are diversities of operations, but it is the same God which worketh all in all." (1 Corinthians 12:4-6)

The one who gives us grace for service is the Holy Spirit. Therefore, we should view no service as different from others (superior or minor). It should not be considered one for glory, the other for subordination, or inferiority.

However, with the anointings we are given, we shall be serving with faith and willingness to work to make God happy in this way; we shall understand this.

"How do I know my anointed service to the Lord?" is a question asked by many Christians, thus, asking how to serve many times. There is one website called *"Got Question,"* which gives a biblical response, and it says:

"No wizard, calculation, or little effort can tell us the anointing. The Holy Spirit distributes as it wills to us (as we find in 1 Corinthians 12:7-11). The common mistake for Christians is trying to serve God in whatever we want to help and test. A spiritual gift doesn't work like that. The calling of God is to serve Him with willingness. He called us to fulfil His Word, but He can enable us in whatever service or gift.

It is possible to delineate spiritual gifts in different ways. If we do it without devoting ourselves too profoundly, the assessment we make to know our capability can show us clearly. When others express it, it can also tell us which one is our anointing. When we serve others, those who watch us and see us doing so can also tell us and differentiate our blessing; it could be something we did not know or did not notice. Prayer is also helpful. The Holy Spirit gives us spiritual gifts and knows what He gave us. We can't ask God how we got it; we shall use it in a better way to serve Him.

God has called some teachers because He anointed them with teaching. God has called them servants because He has blessed them to assist. However, to know our anointing clearly does not mean this will prevent us from serving outside our consecration. Is there any use to knowing what type of anointing He has given us? No need. Is it a mistake to focus on spiritual gifts too much if it distracts us from the chance of providing other services to God? Yes, of course. If God has given us to use us, He will also prepare us to serve Him.

If you do not know yourself adequately, you will find something not to think about or plan for when applying it. If your gifts are not balanced with your role, you will be like a peg in the middle of a circular well. It is, in fact, something hopeless for you and others. Although it gives minimal results, it will waste even the abundant gift and your power.

Do we have a choice for the type of service we give?

Every service member has a preference. We should serve God with the anointing He put in us when He created us. In this regard, if there is anyone who doesn't know what he has in him, he should pray and ask God for it to be revealed or given to him.

Whenever the church deploys people to service, it should confirm that it is in unity with God's assignment. The assistance should not happen by imposition. A Christian who will be assigned must conform, and his consent must be asked for and confirmed before deployment. Serving the Lord must be something the individual has to do for his own sake, but not that he is doing it because the church imposed on him or was elected by members by a majority vote.

God will elect or appoint anybody for service. Because the house owner is God himself, and when He sets someone for assistance, He knows what type of anointing He has given to this specific person. When any service provided is known to come from God, then the role of the congregation is to accept and obey the voice. Sometimes, sound may come not from the heavens but the wrong direction and give assignments which are not correct, from the fleshly will and appoint someone to the lousy service. But the person servicing should try to check if the work given does agree with what he is feeling and agree or disagree with the mandate given without hesitation and let the assigners know what he feels.

"For it is God which worketh in you both to will and to do of his good pleasure." (Philippians 2:13)

This situation should not be looked at as if it is a rejection of the instruction from the leadership. The best thing is to discuss it openly with a positive mind and decide on the best solution with the agreement. The service you are giving is only for the Lord and not anyone else. Thus, we must take it from this point. Anyone serving with an anointing not given from above, most times as observed, becomes fruitless.

One of the reasons people give for not giving service in the house of the Lord is that they do not have the anointing. Nothing can be outside the truth. The problem is being double sided. The first one is people need to have a way to know their talents. Most of the time, people serve without knowing they have an anointing. Secondly, they need to function correctly, trying to synchronise their blessing with the service they give.

Some people are not used to having different types of anointing. The anointed people's talents must be identified: research, writing, sketching a map of the earth, preparing questionnaires, agitating, beautifying, planning, recreation, maintenance, drawing, and cooking.

"And there are differences of administrations, but they all are to serve the same Lord." (1 Corinthians 12:5)

How do we know the service given to us by the Lord?

Although this question seems complicated, a Christian, given the anointing from our Lord Jesus Christ, will have a greater flow of power through him and serve the poor with tangible results (fruits), which is doubtless.

For example: evicting the evil spirit, declaring healing over sickness with confidence in the mighty name of Jesus, the evil spirit will shout and go out, healing will be instant, and recovery will be permanent. This alone is adequate evidence. Anything that arises around the service can be criticised or commented. We shall not be bothered about that so far as we make sure the service we give does not have any problems, but the evil spirit is disturbed and may raise some obstacles, opposition, and testing.

Moving ahead, noticing all these are important. It requires us to be awake, fight with diligence, and stand firm in this situation because the devil tries to raise some obstacles. On this point, church leaders and members must fight evil spirits by delineating with a solid conviction to do some work that has good results. What should be is that members should not be dismayed by gossip and opposition over the Holy Spirit. Instead, they should work by carefully noticing and diligently standing to allow the church service to succeed, strengthen servants of God, and play their share honestly.

Are we fulfilling our part by serving?

As usually observed, Christians know in which service their anointing is and are engaged practically, but they lack serving fully. For this, there are many reasons given as a cause. However, when evaluated correctly, all these reasons cannot justify why they are not serving. Therefore, because these lame excuses do not help, some people trying to exempt themselves from service misjudge.

This type of retreat from giving service is a mistake and we should try to be loyal to the Lord and continue serving the Lord. Those who are in the service may find very testing problems. The problems might be multiple-sided and can start from different directions. Christians need to understand that the problem will come from insiders or outsiders, but in whatever form they are happening, the source, we shall know that it is from the enemy or flesh when we get tired. However, the spiritual fight shall continue by serving, which is something expected from a strong Christian not to cut off service even if the devil fights. Other essential points we see hereunder are which we shall consider.

We shall carefully focus and answer them ourselves to evaluate ourselves. We shall be expecting and asking the Lord what we missed because of what was around us while being prepared to fulfil according to what He said, in His way and assortment, by walking faithfully and allowing it to happen in the Lord's way.

- Do we have the complete will to serve in the house of the Lord?
- Did we notify our church openly about our service burden?
- Are we given service assignments?
- Are we seated disappointed because the church did not give us an assignment, or are we waiting to leave it to the Lord to fulfil?

We can raise these and other questions, evaluate ourselves openly, and with a clear conscience, turn into God's valid will and service, and reach the goal. When we don't do this, we will be damaging ourselves but no one else, and understanding this will help us value the service we are giving at a high price. This will help us strengthen our service and prioritise because nothing is more significant than this. Our effort will be tremendous. It will enable us to support the church as well. The service we give willingly and wholeheartedly will glorify the Lord and make us victorious.

If you are not participating in any service, what type of reason are you giving? Abraham was old, Jakob exploited, Liya was not beautiful, his brothers pushed Joseph, Moses was torturing, Gideon was poor, Samson was dependent, and Rehab was corrupt. David was not honest and had many family problems, Elijah was praying to die, Jeremiah was depressed, and Jona disagreed. Peter was emotional and spontaneous, Martha was stressed, the Samaritan lady had to marry into many unsuccessful marriages, people disliked Zekios, Thomas was suspicious, Paul was sick, and Timothy was shy and cowardly. All the above are different weaknesses. However, God used them for other purposes. So, if you stop giving excuses for not serving, He will use you.

Chapter 10

31. SERVING THE WILL OF GOD

First, it is essential to recognise and understand that serving the godly will is the primary requirement of Christianity. We also need to know that the primary reason for our creation is to do God's will.

And we must know what it means to serve and how it should be. Indeed, the types and quantity of services to God are so numerous that it is impossible to finish explaining here and there. Still, it is possible to give a summarised explanation.

What many people do not understand is the word 'servant'. Many think quickly about stewards, priests, and full-time church ministers when they hear the word 'minister'. But God says that everyone who is in His family is a servant. So, if you are a Christian, you are a minister and you must accomplish your ministry. When Peter's mother-in-law was sick, Jesus healed her. Using the new health she received, "she rose and served them" (Matthew 8:15). It is what we must do. We need to help others and accept them as a blessing. To serve Him as saved: make the tithing, do not sit down and just wait for the Kingdom of the heavens.

We will try to list from the lowest to the highest level (in human terms). So then, with heartfelt love, every one of us receives the service designed by God which is love and glory without regard to individual worldly status.

Many people don't seem to understand this. Yes, it is best to offer a sacrifice of service that is precious to God, which is beautiful, and pleasing to the eyes of men. But is the gift really to serve God's will or something else? God himself sits down on His throne in heaven, and He searches and weighs it. Above all, it is essential to consider pleasing God in the service of doing His will. The word on the sacrifice which shall be to God says:

"Whether there is a blind man, or a broken man, or anyone with a stab wound, or a stumbling block, you shall not offer all these things to God; neither shall you make a burnt offering to God on the altar of fire" (Leviticus 2:22).

When King Saul was ready to offer sacrifices to God, he faced difficulties because he did not do so in what he should have done.

"Samuel said to Saul, 'You have not made it. You have not kept the commandment that Jehovah, your God, has commanded you. So now your kingdom will not stand; Jehovah has chosen a man of his heart, and God has commanded him to be ruler over his people because you have not observed what Yahweh has commanded you'" (1 Samuel 13:13).

King Saul was ruined by not keeping the order of the house of Yahweh, and God took his authority away from him.

Therefore, this mistake was made by not maintaining the statutes of the house of Yahweh. How many times have we let our God down in this way? Perhaps we might have thought it small, or what we thought was simple was not as we thought, but it might have angered God. Therefore, we need to consider it carefully.

We might obey and serve a wealthy man, or an official supposed to benefit us, but it becomes difficult even to greet a friend from whom we did not get any benefit. But a man who gives his goodwill in service to God will have problems as we focus only on those, we base our greetings on those who benefited us. Interestingly, this is very common in the eyes of people. To whom is it best to obey? What if a man chooses to observe someone who, rather than following his God, is temporarily employed and who tomorrow changes and betrays himself, who cannot give even a fraction of God's benefits? It cannot serve or accomplish the will of God beyond obedience. But God says about obedience in His Word:

"And Samuel said, Hath the Lord as great delight in burnt offerings and sacrifices, as in obeying the voice of the Lord? Behold, to follow is better than sacrifice, and to hearken than the fat of rams." (1 Samuel 15:22)

"Not everyone that saith unto me, Lord, Lord, shall enter into the kingdom of heaven; but he that doeth the will of my Father which is in heaven." (Matthew 7:21)

Here the Lord Jesus clarifies how precious it is to do His Father's will. Some foolish ones want to relax and enjoy when they think about what Jesus has done for them.

Then the Lord Jesus made an example for us, and He went away, giving us the commandment, "Do not be weary, for I have finished on behalf of you" (John 16:33). It is our debit record of the sin that Jesus cancelled. He has ascended to his Father's right hand, which we cannot remove with our capacity, but He has accomplished in His divine capacity. He sat on the throne and said He would come again to put us back in the dwelling place He had prepared for us; amen!

Therefore, when we have done His divine will, He who brought us into His glorious kingdom will come again with glory, to take us where He lives, wearing a crown of glory.

Only today, we must make sure we do the will. We can be worthy of the crown of glory in our lives today in this land, living, working, having social relations, our union, our love, etc. If we don't have these, as the Word tells us, our faith is in vain. Because God is not only measuring our trust in His name or how we walk in the church, but the hard work, dedication, actions, and deeds we have shown in our lives to do His will. Jesus said he would not enter the Kingdom of the heavens without fulfilling His commandment. Because we don't have any alternative, our choice can only keep with the Word.

Since we face beyond what we can bear, we must persuade ourselves to carry the load properly. We must consider not trying to shoulder the burden placed on someone else. All we must do is take the same thing given to us. Helping, receiving, caring, being loved, etc., is OK and supported. But it is inappropriate to say that we should bear that burden just because we want to carry it, that it can be overwhelming and ineffective because the Lord did not give us, and that hardship and coercion can happen.

Many have suffered injuries, bruises, failures, etc. Therefore, we need to realise that doing the will is walking according to what He told us. God is not responsible for any hardships we face outside of this. God knows our limitations better than we know ourselves, and we should not try Him. The Lord knows what we will do in due season; identifying and understanding our faithfulness will bless us more as we want to do His will.

Let us read the following example from the Bible. "It will be as if anyone going abroad called his servants and gave them the money he had, and he gave to each according to his capacity; to one five talents, to the other two and the third one he gave one and immediately went abroad. And he that received five talents went and managed to double it for him and gained another five: and he that received two gained another two. But one who received one from him went and dug the earth and buried his master's money in fear of losing even what he had taken. And after a long time, he came back, and he demanded his talents; he gave them together with the profit they gained after trading with the talent they were given when he left. And he that received five talents came near, delivered another five talents, and said, Lord, thou hast given me five talents: behold, I exchanged and gained five more talents, thus have now had ten talents to give you. His master said to him, 'Well done, good and faithful servant. You proved trusted with a little; I will appoint you over many. Enter into the joy of your lord.' And he that received two talents also came near, and said, Lord, thou hast given me two talents: behold, I have gained you another two talents. Thus, I now have four talents for you. His master said to him, 'Well done, good and faithful servant. You proved trusted with a little; I will appoint you over many, enter into the joy of your lord.' And he that received a talent also came near, and said, Lord, I know that thou is a cruel man, reaping, and gathering in which thou hast not sown: and I was afraid, and went and buried thy talent in the earth: behold, thou hast thy talent. In reply, his master said to him, 'Wicked and sluggish servant, if you do you know that I will reap and gather where I did not sow, you should have entrusted my money to the exchangers, and I would have come and taken what I had with the extra money.' Therefore, he ordered his other servants to take the talent from him and give it to the one who had ten talents. Then said for your loyalty, I shall add more for he has doubled his effort, thus to one who has more shall be added, and from the one, he didn't make a profit, even what he has will be taken away" (Matthew 24:14-29).

It requires all the trust and rewards we want to serve God. Serving is a price worth paying. But we must keep within His goal, firmly enduring with His undeserved kindness, not fearing the dust that would provoke an enemy in the way we are going to do His will. Only evangelical patrons who have been able to discourage the enemy through evangelism in preventing the enemy's work will always prevail.

If we sincerely believe that there were saints who loyally served their God amid the times, there is no reason why we cannot serve godly wills as they did by the undeserved kindness that helped them.

Because God, who made them walk in integrity with Him and fulfil His will, is something also possible today. He is impartial and can give us undeserved kindness if we are willing to do so. We are all equal in front of Him. Such truth in the ministry should govern our hearts. As we joyfully come before Him to receive His blessings, we should also be before Him when He is angry. We must reprove, counsel, even give advice, and make our determination to accept what is missing or when our part needs adjusting.

There is no doubt that God will travel with us through the ups and downs. Therefore, we, too, need to make it abundant in unfailing circumstances to please the faithful God, who neither forsakes us nor leaves us, but we also need to keep our eyes, thoughts, and spirit to make our God happy, seeking His face day and night.

The only way to win is through perseverance. Therefore, our steadfast struggle to the point of victory on any battlefield is our dedicated struggle. Between the journeys of triumph, activity, success, and failure, the chance of defeat and success can happen interchangeably. Therefore, it should be an achievable wrestling battle to continue our struggles until we reach the ultimate goal without concentrating on what we have achieved. We can't achieve victory without sacrifice.

While we walk in God's house with other people, the situations mentioned above might happen to us. As we walk in the same way that we walk in the house of God together, as we are multiple, our difference can equally be numerous, making it difficult to know; thus, we can assume that it will make it difficult to know everyone.

Our relationship includes disagreements, pushing, rejection, hatred, strife, reward, etc. Essentially, the cause of these events often comes from the enemy (Satan). Therefore, it is crucial to understand that there are problems with human behaviour, lack of sincerity, incomprehension, and understanding. However, we need undeserved kindness because these conditions are known to our Creator. We are no longer under the law but under His grace.

"For sin shall not have dominion over you: for ye are not under the law, but under grace." (Romans 6:14)

"What then? shall we sin, because we are not under the law, but under grace? God forbid." (Romans 6:15)

Therefore, this explains that we are never allowed to sin because we have His grace. As some have said, if we fall into sin, sin by Christ's death has been cancelled for us who believe in Him, but some may think, 'There is no need to repent, for through his undeserved kindness we have been saved through Christ Jesus,' or say, 'What will happen if we fall in to sin?' There is no need to be worried about what will happen if we sin. We need to be careful because this mental attitude violates the above word in the Bible. Why did He have to come to the earth and die on the Cross for our sake? While the cancellation of our death in Christ redeems us from the sin inherited from Adam, we will receive mercy by repenting before the throne of God for the sins inherited and for the sins that we will commit during the rest of our lifetime. Jesus's death is not a guarantee from our current sin. Still, it is the divine way of escaping eternal death, which has been given us by undeserved kindness as a means of return to our God through confession if we sin.

The Old Testament says we cannot get cleaned from our sins without sacrificing the blood of birds, sheep, goats, and bulls. Jesus freed us from the constant blood sacrifices of any animal. What is great love? Jesus was the only one who could provide that. Let the glory be Jesus of Nazareth, the Son of God, born of the Virgin Mary! Therefore, given the doing of His will, our service to God, who has packed up our work and set us free through His Son Jesus, should be excellent, saving what we can't. Jesus is faithful. He may repay us at the right time for our deserved price, and He will pay us our reward accordingly. As He described it in his word:

"And, behold, I come quickly; and my reward is with me, to give every man according as his work shall be. Amen Jesus will come soon, Maranatha!" (Revelation 22:12)

Returning with true repentance

People can say a lot about repentance, but if we don't know what repentance means, we may take it for granted. Therefore, it is beneficial to understand the nature of repentance in advance.

Instead of someone who says in his call, "I have come to blame you," I may be more attentive to one who says, "I have called to thank you." And such conversation might quickly find our ears and awaken us; it may create a smile in our eyes, but the voices do not come on our choice; some may satisfy us. Now, what is the voice that we need to hear? Repent or rejoice? My friends, true joy comes from true repentance. They will delight with a cry of excitement made in a place where abuse is not there. Repentance is a healthy voice; thus, please talk about repentance.

Repentance is a return, a change of identity, a return from sin. We can refer to repentance in two ways: genuine and sincere, and another may be repentance, of mere pretence or not from the heart.

A return is a return from destruction or error to the actual or the right direction. A transformed identity is a fundamental change from continuing the older person's exercises or doing the older man's job with a new identity: a complete cleansing of sin.

What does the word of God say about repentance? Here are a few:

"Yet if they bethink themselves in the land whither they are carried captive, and turn and pray unto thee in the land of their captivity, saying, We have sinned, we have done amiss, and have dealt wickedly." (2 Chronicles 6:37)

Immediately King Solomon finished constructing the temple of Yahweh. Then, he kneeled before God in front of the people of Israel and prayed as he offered thanksgiving. King Solomon believes that Jehovah God is merciful and forgiving. And he is fully aware of the need for repentance.

Therefore, Solomon, king, prayed before his God, asking for the mercy of his people.

To repent, we must be convinced, regretted, saddened, and determined not to do so again and decide to return. If we go back to the same sins after repenting, it will be counterfeit repentance, which will only pretend to be out of the evil we have repented.

When we approach our God in repentance, we need to be careful not to lie to God, for He knows that we have already repented in true or pretence.

The prophet Isaiah says, "Remember, weep" (Isaiah 46:8). Therefore, he keeps himself away from all avenues and opportunities that could cause him to avoid making a sin-binding mistake.

"Remember this, and shew yourselves men: bring it again to mind, O ye transgressors." (Isaiah 46:8)

Since the point is to return from deep in the heart, we should be sure that we make a determined heartfelt decision when we decide to repent our sins. When we have a life free from sin and reproach, our witness is not only a man but also God, who sees us as exemplary to people. Therefore, the value of our repentance also includes our dedication to the heart, along with change and return.

Another important thing is that we should believe that God is a God of mercy, and He indeed shows mercy and forgives us, accepting and forgiving those who have sincerely brought their sins before Him. But, on the other hand, the enemy can constantly bring to our hearts our sins that we have repented and accepted mercy, causing us to disrupt our peace and lead us into a life of defeat. At this point, we need to understand that this is an enemy's plan and, as the Word says, wipe out our sins, not turn back, knowing that we shall not think about it at all.

"I, even I, am he that blotteth out thy transgressions for mine own sake, and will not remember thy sins." (Isaiah 43:25)

"I have blotted out, as a thick cloud, thy transgressions, and, as a cloud, thy sins: return unto me; for I have redeemed thee." (Isaiah 44:22)

Jehovah clearly states that he will make our sins as clean as the white cloud and redeem us and that He wants us to return to Him. So, our God has made it clear that He does not want us to be lost but always wants us to return.

However, the enemy tries to get us into the trap and make us live a weak life that is defeated, and he tries to make us short of the glory the Lord has designed for us, and he will take us down with him to hell. Therefore, we must abandon sin wholeheartedly and avoid anything that exposes us to sin with a clean heart, in practice, without losing sight of this thought. It is a great reward to return to God's arms in obedience, to our God's compassionate goodwill. May the glory be to our God, who has increased His mercy on us!

If a man cannot repent and return to God's way, he will walk in his way. Therefore, it's impossible to please God while walking in their way. About repentance, this is what the Word says:

"For my thoughts are not your thoughts, neither are your ways my ways, saith the Lord." (Isaiah 55:8)

What we need to do is leave our ways and return to the practice of God. God has not told us, 'I will not bring you back to my way,' and the chances of returning are not closed. God never seeks the destruction of the wicked person. On the contrary, God in His Word says:

"I will seek that which was lost, and bring again that which was driven away, and will bind up that which was broken, and will strengthen that which was sick: but I will destroy the fat and the strong; I will feed them with the judgment." (Ezekiel 34:16)

Therefore, the LORD is righteous in His works and judgements, but our faults, if we remain in our weaknesses, condone ourselves to destruction instead of repenting. Thus, living a clean, blameless life can be as challenging as climbing a big mountain. But as the Lord said to Paul, by his undeserved kindness, he helps us; he makes us able to do what we cannot; the Word says:

"And he said unto me, My grace is sufficient for thee: for my strength is made perfect in weakness. Most gladly therefore will I rather glory in my infirmities, that the power of Christ may rest upon me." (2 Corinthians 12:9)

Because of the weakness of the flesh, if there is nothing that will discomfort it, it will become uncontested and cause us to fall into sin and separate us from our God. It's very easy for flesh revelry and getting off the line when things go wrong. However, it always helps us when our inner spirit strengthens us and when we listen and obey the rebuke of the Holy Spirit.

"What? Know ye not that your body is the temple of the Holy Ghost which is in you, which ye have of God, and ye are not your own? For ye are bought with a price: therefore glorify God in your body, and in your spirit, which are God's." (1 Corinthians 6:19-20)

If we decide to honour the Holy Ghost in us, it must help us to be determined to avoid any sin.

When sin is plotting against us at our doorstep, the Holy Spirit will reprove us before we sin. When we disregard this reproof, which is the will of our flesh, we are sad with the Holy Spirit. But, if we continue to grieve the Holy Spirit, He too will stop reprimanding.

If we stop hearing the reproach of the Holy Ghost and He keeps silent, we may travel as we remain caught with our weaknesses without knowing we are trapped many times. But, on the other hand, if we do not notice that our short-comings and sins are getting more robust against us and we do not repent, our end will be under the control of the enemy devil and to die forever. That is why those who have fallen into sin may continue their path to destruc-tion, even knowing that he has lost, but some will walk to church and may pray for a little; but still, they may not know where they stand.

Since we live in a time of mercy, as opposed to the Old Testament, some will never consider seeking God's mercy; they were walking in the same way because God did not punish them immediately because of their sins. Even when they know that they have sinned, some people do not want to get out of their wrongs because they have persuaded themselves to believe that God has approved them in their status by not punishing them immediately. It will then be a sign of great mercy because the Holy God did not punish them and there will be a price for their sin later.

There may be those who think there is sin that needs repentance and those that don't. But according to the Word of God, all sins need repentance. To do what should not be done and not do what is commanded by the Word of God is sin, not to respect God's law or obey, which is in all the Holy Word. But above all laws, God's Word tells us that unforgiven sin is blasphemy against the Holy Ghost.

"Wherefore I say unto you, All manner of sin and blasphemy shall be forgiven unto men: but the blasphemy against the Holy Ghost shall not get excuse unto men." (Matthew 12:31)

How wise is it to avoid a sin that cannot be repented or forgiven? No matter how much a man knows the Word of God, the knowledge of the word alone has no value unless he practices it in his life and what he has learnt from the Word of God.

When those knowledgeable of the Word want to experience what they think is right in their flesh, they use scripture that tests the Word with their desires. Then, they use it to cover up their mistakes as the right criterion by smartly giving it a different interpretation to support their will. It is a practice that is extremely dangerous and has led to the misguided teaching of many in this era.

Before we can use the Word of God to understand or refer to it, we need to read the overall text of the chapter to get the full content. It is essential to reveal what the Word says, not the context. The Word's context is the content of the message in the chapter, and the addition of self-thought ideas can lead to error; thus, one should carefully express it.

"Therefore say unto the house of Israel, Thus saith the Lord God; Repent, and turn yourselves from your idols; turn away your faces from all your abominations." (Ezekiel 14:6)

If we expose ourselves to such errors and sinful practices, we must repent quickly and return. Failure to do so hurts not anyone but the person who has sinned. The Lord Jesus said that if we did not repent, we would be lost:

"I tell you, Nay: but, except ye repent, ye shall all likewise perish." (Luke 13:3)

His Word reveals how much joy there will be even in heaven for a repentant person:

"I say unto you, that likewise, joy shall be in heaven over one sinner that repenteth, more than over ninety and nine just persons, which need no repentance." (Luke 15:7)

If we look at the scriptures quoted below, we will see how vital repentance is to our lives and how repentant mercy from God will bring forgiveness to our weakened flesh and end our dedication to the blessed one.

Here are a few words mentioned in various Bible passages about the need for repentance:

"Repent ye, therefore, and be converted, that your sins may be blotted out when the times of refreshing shall come from the presence of the Lord; And he shall send Jesus Christ, which before was preached unto you" (Acts 3:19-20)

"And the times of this ignorance God winked at; but now commandeth all men everywhere to repent." (Acts 17:30)

Romans 2:5, "But after thy hardness and impenitent heart treasurest up unto thyself wrath against the day of wrath and revelation of the righteous judgment of God; now commandeth all men everywhere to repent"

"Or despisest thou the riches of his goodness and forbearance and longsuffering; not knowing that the goodness of God leadeth thee to repentance?" (Romans 2:4)

"For godly sorrow worketh repentance to salvation not to be repented of: but the sorrow of the world worketh death." (2 Corinthians 7:10)

"The Lord is not slack concerning his promise, as some men count slackness; but is longsuffering to us-ward, not willing that any should perish, but that all should come to repentance." (2 Peter 3:9)

By water, the body is washed clean, and the blood of Christ cleanses the sin.

True repentance is not only a leaf decorated with words; it is also a fruit that results from the action. It is a return from the path of destruction in which someone has walked in the way of wailing, weeping, regret, and oath (determination). "And the seed of Israel separated themselves from all the strangers" (Nehemiah 9:2). "Let us make a covenant with our God, and let him do according to the law" (Ezra 10:3). John the Baptist did not merely tell people to confess and get baptised in the water for signs. In any effect, they got a convenient list. "He who has two outer garments will share them. Do not take more than you should, and you must not act unjustly. Let your salary be enough for you" (Luke 3:10-14).

If we have genuinely repented in the state of our country's church, we should represent testifying in our behaviour and actions. If we have received false prophesy, we must shut our mouths and speak only the pure Word of God. Suppose we have plundered the people's pockets in the ministry's name using imaginative language, embezzling accumulated money for ourselves. In that case, we must refrain our hearts and our hands together from doing this. If we used to criticise men and our work has become a place of reproach, we should pause and search ourselves with His spirit and word. If we want to listen to anyone's counsel other than our voice, we should say, 'Please advise me.' If we have cultivated the evil traits of a 'strange seed' that is not of God, we should grow the fruitage of the Spirit in its replacement. God beholds all in our hearts, but men need to see the fruit of our repentance revealed.

Practicing the Holy Spirit's gift for the purpose given

The church's total spiritual growth to have spiritual shape and fullness through the Holy Spirit receives different anointings. One who has received a special gift of grace to ensure that he grows, spiritual formation, and fullness must be there. At 1 Corinthians 12:1, Apostle Paul says: "I would like you to know about spiritual things, brothers." Some Bible teachers believe that we should not become ignorant to spiritual gifts. This truth reminds us to have both the gift and the knowledge. Because if you don't have the awareness, it's like peeled-off electrical wire, and if you don't have the skill, it becomes as if you speak any language (for example, Ethiopian), you read but don't write. Seeking the knowledge in using the Holy Spirit's gift in your service depends on what you would like to give to the foundation of your service. I am aware that there is a wide range of differences in the understanding or beliefs about the gifts of the Holy Spirit in much of Christian life.

But it also helps us to know that the Holy Ghost's gift is free. If it is a gift (free), it is not a skill. If it is not a skill, qualifications can never be an act to show who they are; it is good to know that the fruit of the Holy Spirit is one believer's spiritual identity and requires to bear spiritual fruit, the quality of a believer. It is a life that involves the process of producing it (as we find in Galatians 5:22-23). If a person serves only as a gift without fruit, it means driving a car without brakes. Third, it is proper to know that for the assistance of the Holy Spirit, we do not represent the gift of service, the one listed in Ephesians 4:11. Participation of all church members in the church for His kindness is a manifestation of the work of the Holy Spirit, moving them like one man (just like a body). However, the gift of service is a gift that demonstrates Christ's authority over the church.

The gift of grace, and the source of it, is Yahweh. His purpose is to purify the body of those in Christ and spread the good news to all nations' children.

The gift of grace, intended for church service, is not intended to serve the individual but to enable them to do as He pleases.

Whether we understand the purpose of gifts of grace or not, we see some ministers taking advantage of undeserved kindness from Jesus, given as a personal gift and descending it into personally exploiting in their service.

Some use the gift of undeserved kindness as a source of income. Here, these servants are supposed not to ask for money in their ministry but to use their undeserved kindness to pray over water, oil, clothes, etc., and give the service freely. But instead, they sell, then allow the people to give whatever they would like to support them willingly; however, they ask them to pay first for those who come to them in prayer, etc. The genuine concern is that it will continue to be a constant practice affecting the work of the Lord, ending up neglecting those who do not have any to pay and serving the rich people, which is outside the principle.

When Christ Jesus sent the apostles into the ministry, He commanded them:

Matthew 10:8, "Heal the sick, cleanse the lepers, raise the dead, cast out devils: freely ye have received, freely give."

In their ministry, the apostles gave priority and more concern to the church to serve the best, not by accumulating a wealth of their own, but by selling what they had before and giving it to the congregation, covering their expenses and other needs.

"And sold their possessions and goods, and parted them to all men, as every man had need." (Acts 2:45)

"Neither did we eat any man's bread for naught; but wrought with labor and travail night and day, that we might not be chargeable to any of you." (2 Thessalonians 3:8)

If a minister is busy in the gospel ministry without reservation, it is the church's responsibility to cover his food and outer garments. However, it is a tremendous moral fall in the ministry's name if he offers his undeserved kindness to the treasury to negotiate how much he should get.

However, we need to notice that those who are well-moving with their services and those reprimanded in their hearts and willingly contributing with whatever they can afford, shall not be challenging to the church.

Other than these, people who are forced or involved without their will are forced to pay a certain fixed amount for the service they get which contradicts the fact written in the Holy books.

Those who must give service with the anointing they received from the Lord must serve with the blessing they have without the need for making a precondition of being under a church and accepting an assignment the church will give them. When they do this, they must understand they respect God because the gift owner is God Himself.

Nowadays, what is usual practice, and a worldly problem, is that some ministers use their anointing to create an income source; we see they will leave their church and establish their own church to pursue their plans.

The problem is not why the parties planted their church but why they would come out of their previous church. Is there any permission they received? Is it with their last church's will, or have they received a vision from God to do so? Have they been prayed for? Before they left? If prayed? It shall be in harmony with positively agreeing with each other's position. How can God plan to have another church where it shouldn't be? Instead of bringing non-believers to church, why focus on snatching the already saved ones? And consider it as if it is a new church establishment?

"For I will not dare to speak of any of those things which Christ hath not wrought by me, to make the Gentiles obedient, by word and deed, Through mighty signs and wonders, by the power of the Spirit of God; so that from Jerusalem, and round about unto Illyricum, I have fully preached the gospel of Christ. Yea, so have I strived to preach the gospel, not where Christ was named, lest I should build upon another man's foundation: But as it is written, To whom he was not spoken of, they shall see: and they that have not heard shall understand." (Romans 15:18-21)

In the twenty-first century, the world's Christian ministers are planting a world-class new branch of church, not following the principles that the apostle Paul wrote and told the Romans about. Still, people continue nowadays by the problems and disagreements in the past, and by thinking that I have better grace, I can plant a church on my own. Such evil practices need to be controlled by mature thinking, for it is inappropriate.

The establishment of the newly planted church should be in the same way that the love and unity of the spirit are maintained to promote the good news of the Kingdom with love and brotherhood with the church of the former local branch.

Since the work is to God's house, it should be viewed carefully and handled with a sincere dialogue, not in a harsh and hostile way or out of concern for the earthly good.

Ministers are to serve according to their gift of undeserved kindness so that the Lord can adequately honour him and apply what he would like to do. But to do so, there should never be fights, arguments, hatred, or separation.

Servants of God should practice glorifying the Lord correctly and applying the way the Lord wants. But to perform this, they should never go into disagreement, quarrel, debate, and separation. The gift of grace stands out when each believer begins to be moved by the undeserved kindness he has received. Grace's influence increases from the Creator, and its fruit becomes known because they have been able to serve with the bit of opportunity they were given to perform.

Today, the world's so-called great servants do not pop up in one day as mushrooms grow suddenly. However, their contributions are insignificant. But because they have little confidence in their ministry, they become what they are. Therefore, we must move with little faith in the grace we have got; however, if we do not, we will face the fate of the enslaved person who hid the talent.

Some believers hide their anointed service for various personal reasons and sit idle. However, every believer has a call, so he must respect the call and move to gain it with his talent. If the Lord suddenly arrives without us ministering what we received, we will lose what we have not done as the lazy servant did. Since there is not a second chance, the fate of this servant is sure (as written in Matthew 25:15-30). Therefore, may God protect us from being like a lazy servant because of the slack to do His assignment.

The issue needs not escape without using those members' gifts with visible anointing, knowing they can give Mat. 25 service. Still, church leaders, stewards, and elders who do not bring them into the ministry or provide them with the opportunity to serve might affect their future. At the same time, they have apparent undeserved kindness from parishioners in the church; while they know that they can do it, their time elapses without fulfilling.

It is for various reasons, primarily because it could be a lack of trust from leaders in the believer, a question of his readiness for service, or a minor indifference of the member to one occasion, such as that the person is not qualified for service, etc.

As a result, there may be a problem preventing them from regaining access to the ministry. Many might have been affected because of such reasons and ended up depressed.

This situation must be discerned, for its structure is damaging not only to the believer but also to the work of the house of God, therefore, it requires careful attention. Fasting and praying for those whose favour is evident in the ministry is the church's primary responsibility and is fully dedicated to the service. It is the sacred duty and responsibility of those who took the assignment to serve loyally and honestly the ministry by remembering their religious commitment.

If these two conditions fail, there will always be trouble. A balanced amount of diligence and willingness must accompany loyalty and turn into action. When that happens, leaders—whether they are servants or isolated—will be able to fulfil their responsibilities.

As humans, believers who render service with extraordinary undeserved kindness may be misguided for the lack of understanding, maturity, and the way they understand and communicate what the Holy Spirit operates beyond their comprehension. Therefore, trying to see how the mistake could have happened and correcting it with sincerity is a priority before rushing to condemn it when an error occurs.

The longer they remain in the ministry, and the more they experience it, the more they will accurately communicate and serve God's will, His will, His revelation, His voice, and the signs.

If they don't have experience in the ministry, it is appropriate to provide upbuilding and encouraging training and support to help them mature. Still, leaders should closely monitor the knowledge and maturity of ministers and must train them finely and faithfully.

Walking in faith, determined

1 Corinthians 15:1-4 says, "I urge you, brothers, to the good news that I preached to you and to whom you received and also to whom you stood, that you might get saved throughout. If not, unless you betrayed the first thing I preached to you. I gave you what I received; I said: 'As the Book says, Christ died for our sins, he died, and on the third day, according to the Book, He rose.'" In short, this is the foundation of Christianity. Christianity is more focused on relationships than other religious practices or other beliefs explain. Instead of listing these as 'do and do not' instructions, the Christian goal encourages a close relationship with God the Father. In the Christian life, this connection became a reality through the work of Jesus Christ and the service of the Holy Spirit. In this relationship, there is also a promise from God that all believers are waiting to go to Heaven.

"For the grace of God that bringeth salvation hath appeared to all men, Teaching us that, denying ungodliness and worldly lusts, we should live soberly, righteously, and godly, in this present world; Looking for that blessed hope, and the glorious appearing of the great God and our Savior Jesus Christ; Who gave himself for us, that he might redeem us from all iniquity, and purify unto himself peculiar people, zealous of good works." (Titus 2:11-14)

We shall live by faith and endurance, the life of righteousness and holiness as we await the blessed hope.

CHAPTER 11

32. LET US CHECK OUR RELATIONSHIP WITH CHURCH LEADERS

We need to keep the relations between the believers and the church leaders healthy. They deserve it. The church leaders are the guardians of God's people, and pastors are shepherds and have a relationship with the Holy Spirit. They deserve it. The connection is not the type of boss and subordinate but that of brotherhood and sisterhood; it should depend on brotherhood and sisterhood. Inside the church leadership, others should humbly carry out their ministry. A servant who likes to be great, as his Word says, must humble himself and feel like he is below.

"But it shall not be so among you: but whosoever will be great among you, let him be your minister." (Matthew 20:26)

Yahweh appoints the heads of the house of Yahweh. Everyone must serve Him by His grace; the Christian must act in his appropriate place. In God's house also, there are service levels at home. Church elders are overall administrators.

In this regard, there are churches with exceptional organisations. Along with those who lead the church members, others may be appointed in the corresponding service or assigned to the posted roles. But they are all servants of the house of Yahweh, not rulers or bosses. It should be well known to all believers. It should never be avoided, rejected, and despised between the believers and ministers. It is a situation that needs to be very careful. Serving the Lord's House in honour, receiving, and uniting is the highest standard for all ministers.

In a church establishment, the person who received the vision from God first and found it accordingly should be a visionary. This visionary will form an elder committee, selecting men working with him and seeking the congregation's opinions. This visionary serves as a regular church leader with the assigned elders. For he is a vision recipient rather than an appointed or elected elder. Elders of the church are nominated and set in church based on the word of God, not by choice, as revealed in the book of Titus.

"For this reason, I have left thee in Crete, that thou mayst organize the rest of the city, and appoint the elders, as I commanded thee: if there be any man that is not accused, and is the husband of one wife, and has believing children, and not charged with divorce or disobedience, appoints him." (Titus 1:5-6)

These are used as principles to appoint church leaders. The service years is not given in the word: but the individual may terminate his service because of sin (by the corruption of an evident lack of righteousness and holiness among the appointed members, health problems, inability to be present because of work, demands of resignation on his own, or the gathering of himself to the Lord.)

The congregation can choose a successor for church elders if someone must be replaced for various reasons based on the constitution; the proper procedure is to appoint those members who are nominated from the congregants' comments.

Church members (the faithful) are the appointed church leaders and ministers (elders, pastors, deacons, apostles, teachers, evangelists, etc.) Therefore, they should obey and respect them. The faithful man understood the importance of submitting to and respecting the servants God had placed in His place. It does not mean that there will be an interim and hard relationship, but ministers need to serve the flock with a humble head, as Christ humbled Himself, and humbly and sincerely, believing that God has placed them in the faith.

Leadership needs to accomplish what pleases God by creating a healthy relationship that stems from sincere and humble spiritual respect on either side. We can take it as problematic. It turns out that this is a mistaken one in both cases. However, it must be corrected, not to remain silent, but to be corrected before it can take root and cause another unwanted problem.

Those under church leadership must avoid such problems and walk by submitting to the Word and listening to the Holy Spirit rather than their fleshly feelings. Because the Holy Ghost gives the power of understanding and wisdom,

"That the God of our Lord Jesus Christ, the Father of glory, may give unto you the spirit of wisdom and revelation in the knowledge of him." (Ephesians 1:17)

"In whom are hidden all the treasures of wisdom and knowledge." (Colossians 2:3)

It protects us from being in trouble by being guided by the thoughts of our flesh. And disobedience to the voice of the holy spirit is not spiritual, so there is a problem.

It serves the enemy's point of attack but also for it. Therefore, we must practice listening to the Holy Spirit.

There are often inconsistent procedures and individual sensitivity in the church. Therefore, do we consider having caused unwanted destruction to God's house by growing into conflicts and problems that are unnecessary unless they are required? Essentially, it is profoundly embarrassing and tragic that such a situation has developed in the house of the Great God, Jehovah.

Some seem insensitive, even to the problems they have caused. Understanding that this results from not maturing, even mentally and in words, is essential. And avoiding this should be the responsibility of each believer. Although God is forgiving and merciful, He is also jealous of His glory and name, but we must know that He does not tolerate the destruction of His house and His glory. Therefore, when He rises, we must be careful in advance to save ourselves from His wrath, knowing that no one can stop Him.

"For our God is a consuming fire." (Hebrews 12:29)

If they have sinned and God has delayed or remained silent, it is invaluable to be careful that no one will continue to do so; we should not think that the delay in the destruction does not mean their sin was scrapped or that God has supported them. On the contrary, our repentance toward Him and our not continuing in our sins will be a way of explaining the glory and love we give to our compassionate God and the fear of Him.

It is crucial to observe the church's unique programs. The vanity of one's service is to honour the Lord and do the works that His Word gives us. Therefore, failure to respect His ministry implies that we do not respect the Lord similarly.

In many places today, this problem seems to be growing in the vicinity of churches. Not respecting time, being absent from the church, having the courage for sinning in the house of the Lord, teaching false doctrine in the gospels, wrong predictions, free service to cleanse the body of Christ, sex, failure to engage in a prayerful schedule, to fail to serve or to accept assignments when called upon to do, to inflame people with accents and gossip, to incite violence against church ministers, to despise and reject the direction from the Church, etc. The Bible's answer to these and many other problems are happening. From this point, it is understandable that the church's existence is under danger. Let us examine the following questions.

As the Word says, this is how we should exercise self-control:

"In all things shewing thyself a pattern of good works: in doctrine shewing uncorruptness, gravity, sincerity, Sound speech, that cannot be condemned; that he that is of the contrary part may be ashamed, having no evil thing to say of you." (Titus 2:7-8)

- What should we do to avoid the problems described above?
- How do we get out of this situation?
- Why do we not come to church on time?
- Have we ever participated in all the programs that the church has prepared?
- Do we respect? Can we?
- The Head of the congregation is Christ, so do we observe obedience and respect the congregation programs as obedience and honour to Christ?
- Do we understand the harm and the destruction of failure to do this?
- To whose benefit are we doing it? Who will be hurt?
- Do we respect church ministers and leaders?
- If we see fault with the leaders or the servants, do we openly point it out and try to advise them, or do we tell others?
- And in doing so, will we be pleasing to the Lord?
- Do we understand the damage resulting from not correcting errors in time?
- Do we try to do it with patience, pure spirituality, and quietness in any discussion and communication,

- or are we acting spontaneously, thinking fleshly, and acting anyhow?
- A spiritual man is led by the Holy Spirit when in one incidence, provoked, agitated, etc.; how do we deal with things?
- As spiritual people, how do we react to such situations?
- Because of this, consider the following word: "See that none render evil for evil unto any man; but ever follow that which is good, both among yourselves, and to all men." (Thessalonians 5:15)
- Do we follow what the Holy Spirit advises us or our fleshly motive in any situation we face?
- What does it mean to have self-control?
- What implication does it have over our relationship with people who administer the house of God?

"But the fruit of the Spirit is love, joy, peace, longsuffering, gentleness, goodness, faith." (Galatians 5:22)

"And to knowledge temperance; and to temperance patience; and to patience godliness." (2 Peter 1:6)

Some members of the church did not behave in the same way. These human characters exist in social relationships, where psychologists and researchers study and validate them. God created man in His likeness and image, but in His flesh, He made us be distinct from each other, that does not have one to be the beauty of His social connections. Thus, man's qualities are listed below:

- Clear, straightforward, bold, sanguine
- Mix, lenient, versatile, melancholy

- Angry, responsive, hasty, choleric
- Cooperative, caring, mentor, mild, phlegmatic

Some may have a mixture of two personalities. For example, they assign these four qualities to eight places. That means a character created by pairing two. And this behaviour is often evident in social life relationships. Since these traits are visible to all humans, the assumption is that no one will be outside them.

Knowing these human behaviours is invaluable to both ministers and leaders. Because if they know, the characteristics of the people they serve will help accommodate each one according to his character/personality and avoid unnecessary conflicts and disagreements. For example: When a courageous and open person expresses his feelings, he can patiently listen and return if his character becomes known. If the angry and resentful one gets up and gets numb, calmly listens, and calmly discusses it. Likewise, it enables others to be like their personality.

Because of the believers, if they recognise and understand these qualities between leaders and ministers, they can approach and discuss them according to his understanding, accepting the ministry they want without conflict and unnecessary trial and misunderstanding.

Church leadership and governance should always be healthy and fit for the faith. Those who run the church should be honest and good examples, strengthening the union of the holy ones by their example and governing. Essentially, the presence of the Spirit of God in the congregation calls for the heart of the people before Him, God the Father, God the Son, and God the Holy Spirit, in the unity of the soul. It will occur when God's people are loved, anointed, cared for, sanctified, and walk in righteousness. The answer is yes. There should never be anything evil in the crowd. Even if there is a problem, efforts should be to fix it as soon as possible. It can happen when sincere, clear contact lines should be on either side. A brother and sister should be in the middle of no more than direct contact, superiority, subordinate, or commanding and obedient. It should have a vital tool of civil respect.

Believers should maintain the respect and obedience of church leaders. Without it, the anarchy of the relationship of command and order can develop into a chaotic, messy situation that will intrude on God's house and its dignity in general. Everyone needs to avoid this because the damage can encompass everyone, not just specific people.

Some members will be irreversible and reject counsel and discipline when they are steadfast in their stand and may not want to use the time of care given to them to return. Such members may be subjected to action until they are entirely cancelled from church membership, according to God's Word, for it says:

"Moreover if thy brother shall trespass against thee, go and tell him his fault between thee and him alone: if he shall hear thee, thou hast gained thy brother. But if he will not hear thee, then take with thee one or two more, that in the mouth of two or three witnesses every word may be established. And if he shall neglect to hear them, tell it unto the church: but if he neglect to hear the church, let him be unto thee as a heathen man and a publican." (Matthew 18:15-17)

When this is a problem among members, the church should follow the same principle. It must work if a statute of limitations is in the church. Given the house of God, His glory, and His flock. If such a person repents, confesses, regrets, and demands the fruit of this fruit in his life, the church may welcome him back once he has confirmed his transformation. The church must protect it because the Lord has paid the price to lose no one. If anyone wants to turn back from the path of destruction and be corrected, you must help him return by doing what is necessary, as long as he wants to return to his God with regret. The Lord has spoken in his Word:

"All that the Father giveth me shall come to me; and him that cometh to me I will in no wise cast out." (John 6:37)

The church should keep that promise, for it says: "You must keep your word" (1 Timothy 6:14).

When a church disciplines its members—obey

An army performs well and fulfils the task when built with solid discipline. Likewise, schools succeed when teachers teach their pupils theory and bring them up, teaching them life discipline. It's not suitable for students to learn without practicing their study subjects. Likewise, parents should be well-disciplined, administering appropriate discipline, counsel, and punishment when they make mistakes; otherwise, they will destroy their children. If they don't, the children inevitably become horizontally corrupt.

Finally, an institution will not succeed without the proper discipline to meet the goal that an institution stands for.

Discipline is also an essential factor in the life of the church. The church deserves to raise the lives of believers in care by building them up in the Word of God and discipline. The ministry isn't just about bringing the lost ones to Christ with the gospel. Since Christ is the Christian goal, He must make the lives of believers grow, being modelled, and built up, according to the counsel of His Word. Since discipline is part of the way the church shapes the lives of believers, it should get a proper place in the life of the believers.

It is rare to find a caring church controlling its congregants from trespassing against Christian discipline. It is not because the church in the Christian morality has well-governed members. But because we find that the people respect the gospel, it is that believers' moral that is dwindling from time to time, and there is no change in the life of the people in the eyes of unbelieving factions. The other point is that the disciplinary process is another case that requires respect and checking oneself to get out of the mistake, but rather try to depart from the disciplining church and join another one. When pastor Dr Tesfa Workineh explains this matter to you, he says:

"Today, the church must discipline its members, but this doesn't work everywhere, especially outside Ethiopia. The reason they neglect discipline is as varied as the churches. Many believers do not practice disciplinary practices in some places because they fear losing their members to another church if they are disciplined. Essentially, this and other reasons should not prevent the church from exercising its authority over Christians and correcting its children. Discipline is the church authority to discipline wrongdoers" (Matthew 18:15-20; 1 Corinthians 5:12-13).

If disciplined, some leave their churches and move to another one. Such a step would leave the man or woman in a weak spiritual state. Those who hear their history will not gain anything, but it will be a stumbling block.

When church members receive disciplinary measures, they should know it is their advantage. They should sit down and examine the cause for the last weakness, renew with confession, and humble themselves to ask how they have trespassed. Then, if they don't have any problem related to other people and if the problem was affecting the house of the Lord, they should ask the congregation and God and correct their life and continue their Christian life. It is the responsibility they must fulfil as Christians.

Let's check ourselves if we have respected church leaders!

"And we beseech you, brethren, to know them which labor among you, and are over you in the Lord, and admonish you; And to esteem them very highly in love for their work's sake. And be at peace among yourselves." (1 Thessalonians 5:12-13)

"Let the elders that rule well be counted worthy of double honour, especially they who labour in the word and doctrine." (1 Timothy 5:17)

"I beseech you, brethren (ye know the house of Stephanas, that it is the firstfruits of Achaia, and that they have addicted themselves to the ministry of the saints) that ye submit yourselves unto such, and to everyone that helpeth with us, and laboureth." (1 Corinthians 16:15-16)

God has appointed ministers who 'preside for good' in the church and are 'weaned in teaching and preaching.' Every believer should be obedient to them. Young people need to be respectful to older ones. The apostle urges Corinthians to especially respect such ones as Stephen, born out of the early temples believing in the excellent gospel in Achaia, and eager to serve the holy ones with much humility.

David once submitted to The Highest, to Saul, knowing that God had taken the kingdom from him, but did not despise Him; he was obedient to Saul until God brought him on the throne. Later, he did not dare to demolish Saul's increasingly powerful position.

In church, when we are with our spiritual leaders, our relationship should be according to the Word of God, full of fear of God, and it is compulsory to be with respect in brotherhood. If we do anything outside this, it might tarnish the name of God and the truth the Gospel has. Therefore, let us check our relationship with our leaders.

33. LET US EXAMINE OURSELVES IF WE ARE RESPECTING OUR CHURCH LEADERS

"And we beseech you, brethren, to know them which labour among you, and are over you in the Lord, and admonish you; And to esteem them very highly in love for their work's sake. And be at peace among yourselves." (Thessalonians 5:12-13)

"Let the elders that rule well be counted worthy of double honour, especially they who labour in the word and doctrine." (1 Timothy 5:17)

God governs the church and teaches and appoints ministers who are wary of preaching. All believers should submit to them. Young people need to obey the older ones. In his message to the Corinthian congregation, the Apostle, believing in the gospel of Achaia as he consults to serve the born again, and the saints with great humility, exhorts Stephen to be respectful to him.

At one point, David surrendered his position to Saul. Later on, he did not dare to overthrow Saul's declining authority. According to the spiritually world, how glorious is the mission? It should not be underestimated. Insulting speaking on it robs us of spiritual power.

Not knowing, we might disturb them. Whoever presents himself like this could not reflect the right way. He should stop and try to check himself and return to the right way.

Leaders may sometimes drop down from their spiritual stance; however, we shall leave their issues to God and keep obeying them.

The priest Eli talked to the lady Hannah saying: "When is your drunkenness going from you? Let your win depart from you," as mentioned in 1 Samuel 1:13-18 when he rebuked her in his speech that is far from humbleness, she did not respond rudely. Still, she responded to him politely that she was not such a type of woman.

"Now Hannah, she spake in her heart; only her lips moved, but her voice was not heard: therefore Eli thought she had been drunken. And Eli said unto her, How long wilt thou be drunken? put away thy wine from thee. And Hannah answered and said, No, my lord, I am a woman of a sorrowful spirit: I have drunk neither wine nor strong drink, but have poured out my soul before the Lord. Count not thine handmaid for a daughter of Belial: for out of the abundance of my complaint and grief have I spoken hitherto. Then Eli answered and said, Go in peace: and the God of Israel grant thee thy petition that thou hast asked of him. And she said, Let thine handmaid find grace in thy sight. So the woman went her way, and did eat, and her countenance was no more sad." (Samuel 1:13-18)

In the priest's speech, Eli was not deserving and was judging her, but Hannah did not give him an answer with a similar tone. So, he was misusing the power, but she respected him and endowed to him by God. So, her response was full of respect. The amazing thing was that after Eli heard what she said, he blessed her and sent her off, and her years of prayer got a response.

Discipline should return to God's will and mind. We should also work hard while we still have the time now and ask for forgiveness from God for our sins. Instead of growing up in our ego in our family, our union, we should care for ourselves before we get irritated.

"Let us search and try our ways, and turn again to the Lord. Let us lift our heart with our hands unto God in the heavens." (Lamentations 3:40-41)

To examine and search our paths in this book: Chapter One: To begin, let us start by reviewing our journey until now, in which we can adjust our ways of seeing how we should walk in God's house, to test our current situation and correct our way. Chapters two and three talk about our relations with our brethren and non-believers. Chapter four reflects on what our social life is like, encouraging us to stop for a while and see how it looks. Chapter five deals with how to look at our relationship with the Lord. Chapter six reflects on avoiding the harmful traditions that we have kept with our Christian life. Chapter seven focuses on understanding what a nation longing for God should do. Chapter eight mainly reflects on our reliance on the word of God. Chapter nine asks us to pause and examine our ministry, and how we are able to serve the will of God. Chapter ten is about doing the will of God, and another chapter talks about how to test our we discuss the problems of being personal, family, community, church reform, to touch the light of the word of our living God, and to be where we are supposed to be.

"Turn thou us unto thee, O Lord, and we shall be turned; renew our days as of old." (Lamentations 5:21)

CHAPTER 12

CONCLUSION

"Let us search and try our ways, and turn again to the Lord. Let us lift up our heart with our hands unto God in the heavens." (Lamentations 3:40-41)

Being a follower of Christ is a great call that touches human life to get to know the Son of God is the Source of life, is accepting life, "the one who has the Son has life" (1 John 5:12). It introduces God, who appeared in a human form but not inheriting religion, nor by registering to be a church to be a member but has a connection and a live attachment to God. A new life develops from this relationship—an active life that grows and matures. When he loses the clean food he can produce, his attachment to the trunk of his lifeline becomes dull, but when he becomes infected with some toxic substance, he becomes stumped, surging, and depleting instead of growing.

Today, this evangelical community has come to a questionable level, both private and social. Although the good news in the holy life starts in righteousness, conduct, good morals, testimony, and love, it has become known for its shocking moral failures, broken unity, distorted living, and resulting disorder (Matthew 18:15-20; 1 Corinthians 5:12-13).

When the church disciplines members, some might leave; this action will affect the people left and their life affected for no value. Their life will not have a good lesson to learn; it might be discouraging.

When the church disciplines members, they need to know it is for the good of them; they should then sit down and examine, renew with confession, ask forgiveness, and if there is any person not ready to ask forgiveness, those who trespassed him and humble himself or could not understand this and mix themselves with the congregation as Christians, then that will be a problem.

www.ingramcontent.com/pod-product-compliance
Lightning Source LLC
Chambersburg PA
CBHW021430150726
47989CB00001B/185